Tom Wolfe Carves Bottlespirits & Neckhangers

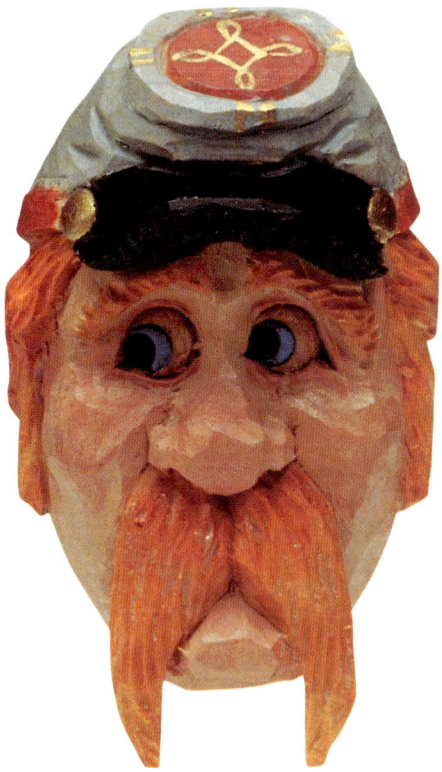

Tom Wolfe

Text written & Photography by
Molly Higgins

Schiffer Publishing Ltd®

4880 Lower Valley Road, Atglen, PA 19310 USA

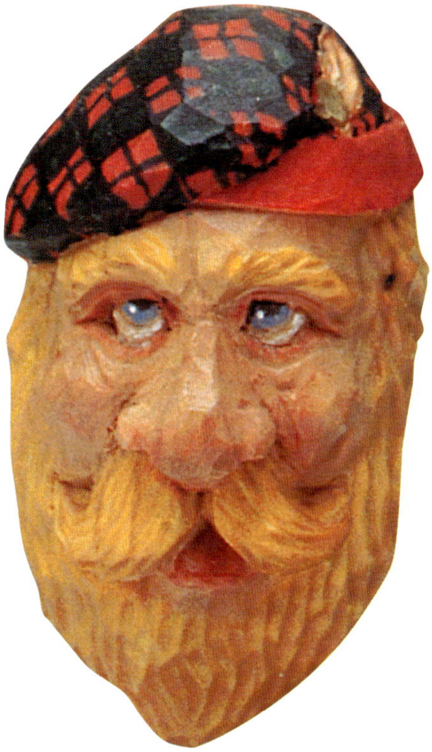

Contents

Library of Congress Catalog Card Number: 98-87840

Book Designed by Randy L. Hensley
Type set in Times New Roman

ISBN: 0-7643-0735-5
Printed in China

Published by Schiffer Publishing Ltd.
4880 Lower Valley Road
Atglen, PA 19310
Phone: (610) 593-1777; Fax: (610) 593-2002
E-mail: Schifferbk@aol.com
Please visit our web site catalog at **www.schifferbooks.com**

This book may be purchased from the publisher.
Include $3.95 for shipping.
Please try your bookstore first.
We are interested in hearing from authors
with book ideas on related subjects.
You may write for a free catalog.

In Europe, Schiffer books are distributed by
Bushwood Books
6 Marksbury Rd.
Kew Gardens
Surrey TW9 4JF England
Phone: 44 (0)181 392-8585; Fax: 44 (0)181 392-9876
E-mail: Bushwd@aol.com

Introduction

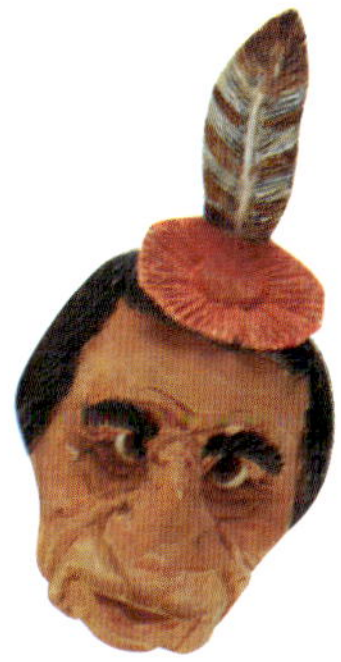

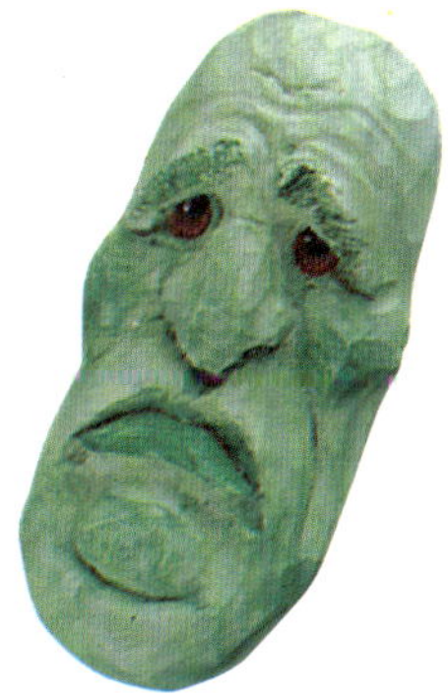

What's in the bottle?

There's something very peculiar about glass bottles. Each one has its own personality. Most of us have at least a couple in our home that we've saved—to use again, as a souvenir, or just because they make neat decorations. Each one has its own personality. Some are cheerful and pleasant; perfect for a bunch of wildflowers. Sometimes they have a streak of mischief inside that can lead to real trouble. Why was it that Alice drank from the little bottle that pushed her through the door into Wonderland? Why do so many people blame their sorrow on the "bottle," but go back to it again and again?

Simple—the spirits.

Bottle spirits swirl around in bottles of all kinds. Sometimes they glimmer in the glass. You can always hear them if a breeze or your breath passes over the top of the bottle. But it's not too often that they show their faces. So how do you know at first glance what's *really* inside a bottle?

The Southern Black slave community had the right idea when they molded faces on their clay bottles. Some were sweet and gentle. Others were mean and ugly, meant to frighten curious children away from finding out that there was even more nastiness inside the bottle.

It's up to you to figure out what sort of spirits are living in your bottles. Then you can go about carving faces to match their personalities, so that unwary visitors to your home can tell right away what lurks in each and every one.

You can even carve the same kind of faces to show everyone what kind of spirits are swirling around in you! An extra little bit of wood on the back of your bottle spirit makes a neck hanger that can warn or welcome, but will always start a conversation.

From an artistic point of view, these bottle spirits are perfect for learning more about carving faces, whether you like them realistic or in caricature. There are enough similarities between the spirits carved in this book to learn the basic approach to carving a face, and enough differences so that you can get a flavor for the endless possibilities you have. Each project can be completed in just a few hours, depending on how much detail you're aiming for. They're also a good way to make use of scrap wood left over from other projects.

If you decide to mess around with bottles, just remember that the spirits aren't always what they seem, and that you may be in for a real surprise!

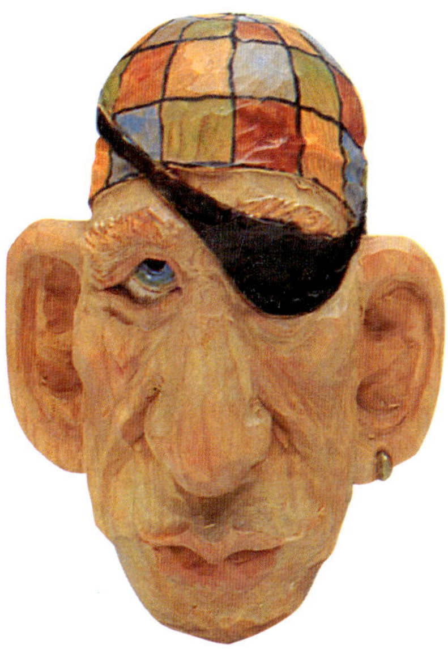

The Carving Process.

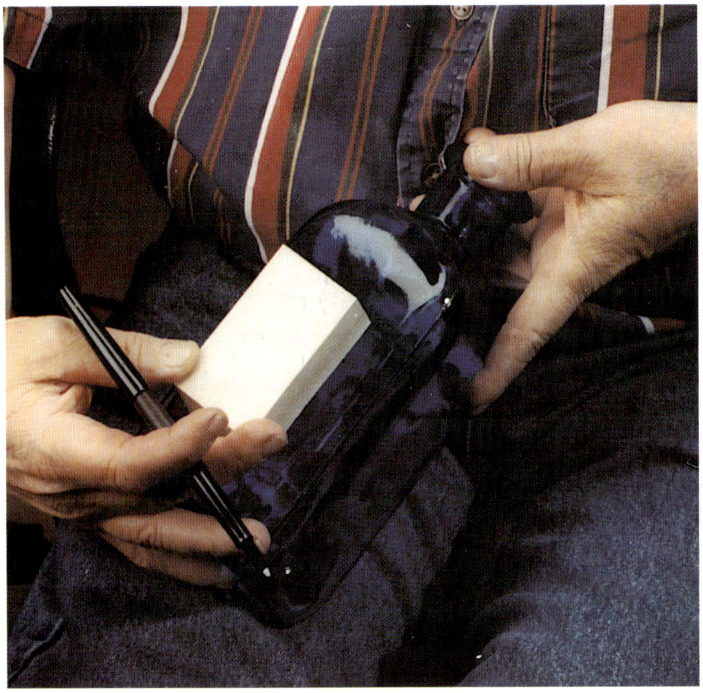

When you're beginning your bottle spirit, it helps to have a bottle already picked out—that way you can size it.

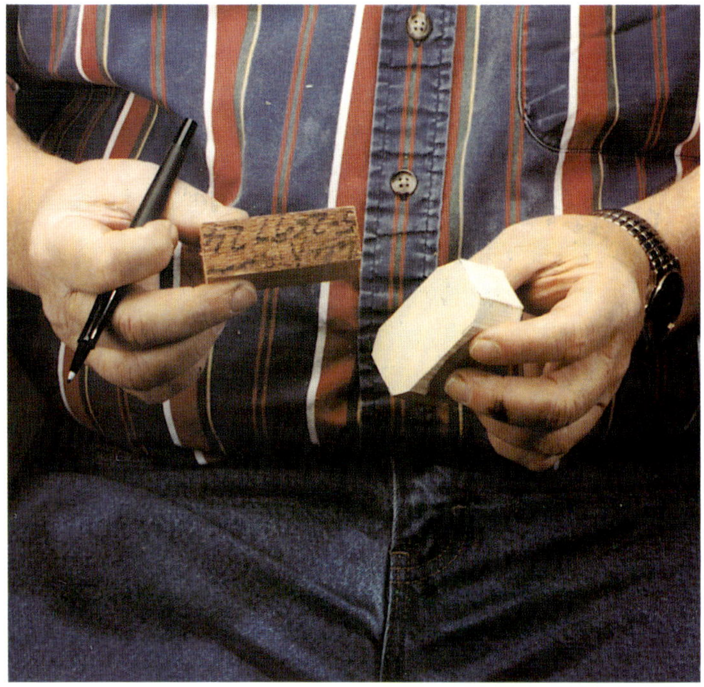

I cut the block down to size on the bandsaw, and cut off the corners while I was at it. This other piece will be the handle.

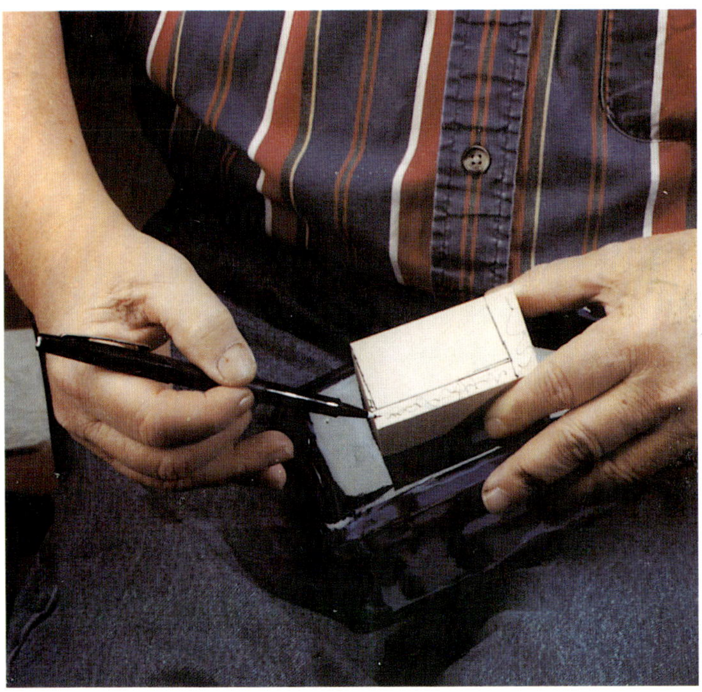

This piece of basswood is a little big for this blue bottle. I'm marking the new dimensions.

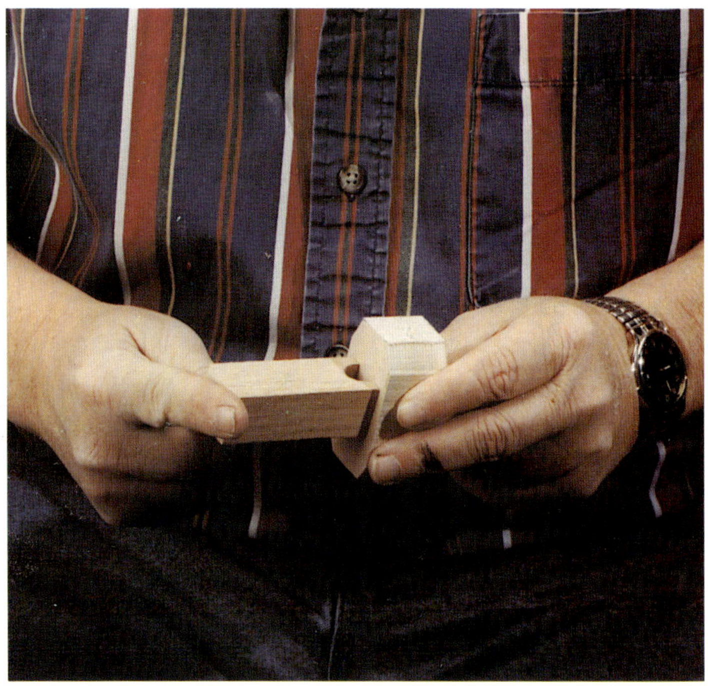

If you want a neck hanger, make sure you cut an arch to allow the ends of your tie or bandana to go through. Glue it like this.

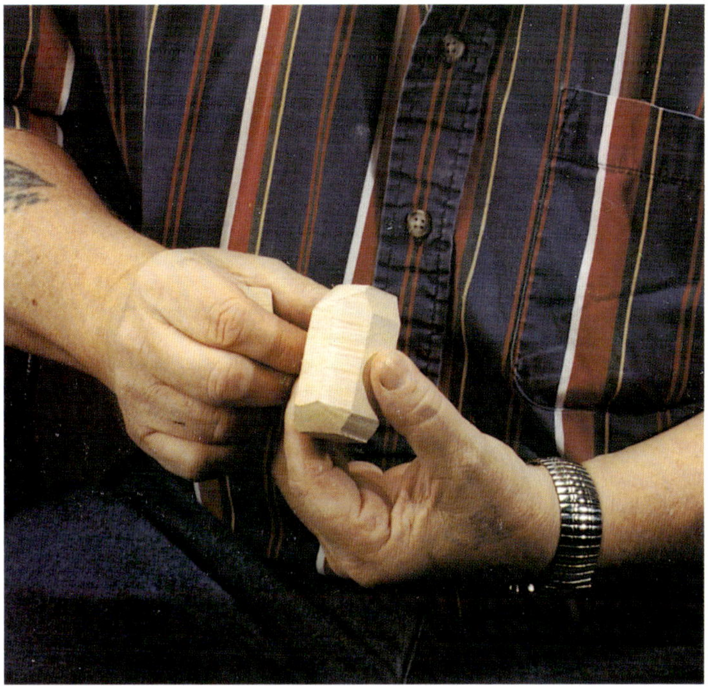

On the head piece, I am cutting the corners off again at a 45° angle to make it look like this. It's just as quick to do it with a knife.

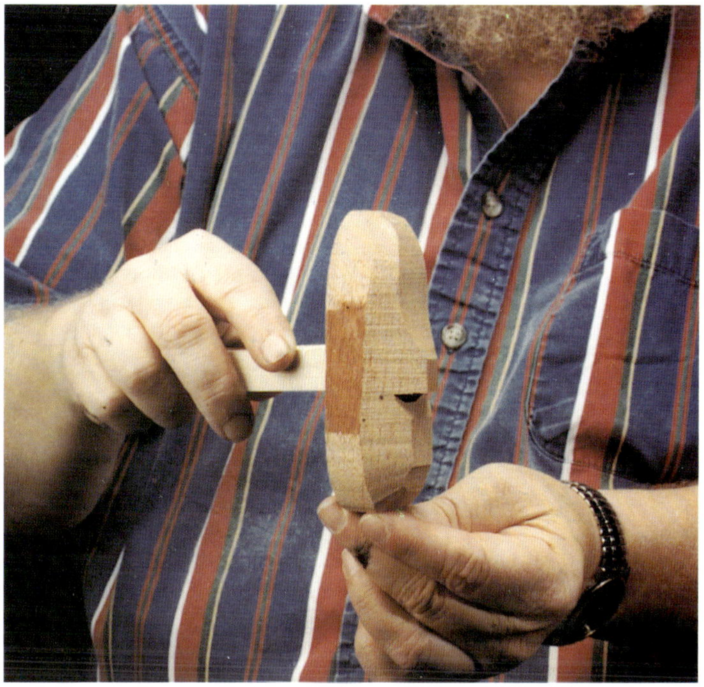

Here's a mahogany piece that's at about the same point as our first one. The only difference is that I've carved a rough profile in it after taking the corners off.

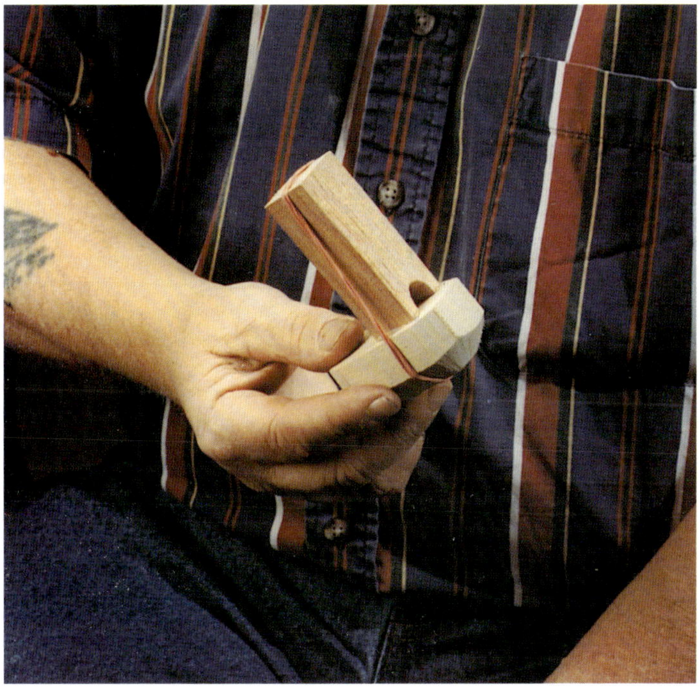

I've glued the handle in place and secured it with a rubber band. It needs plenty of time to dry, so we'll go work on something else for a while.

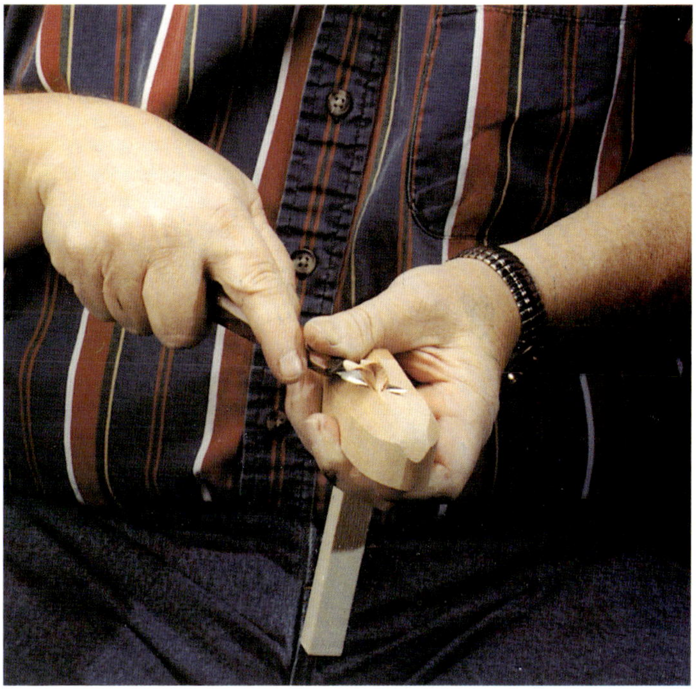

For the face I'm beginning with the nose. I need to first establish a flat plane around it.

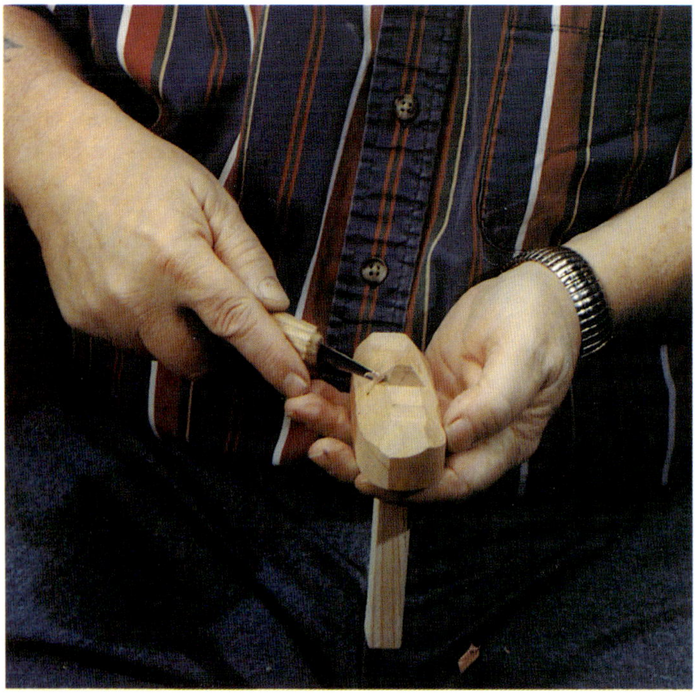

I'm nipping off the corners of the nose at a 45° angle. Cut down to the surface of the face. The nostrils will go here.

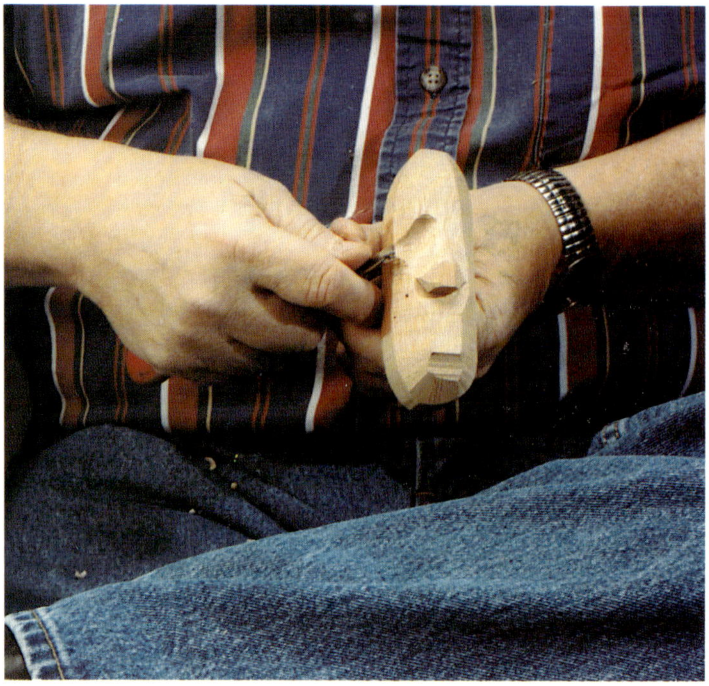

Bring it upwards to hollow out the eye socket.

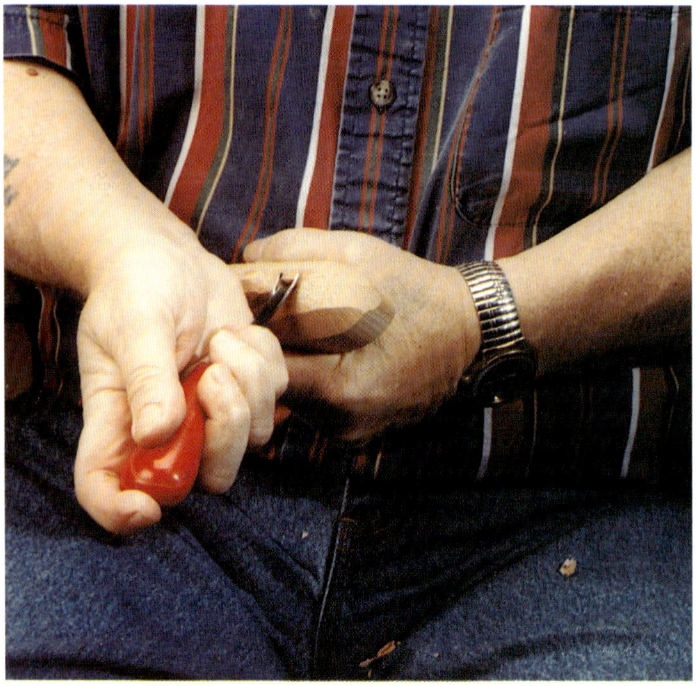

With a gouge, I'm starting from the center and scooping out a pocket in each direction. This helps define the nose, cheekbones, and eyes.

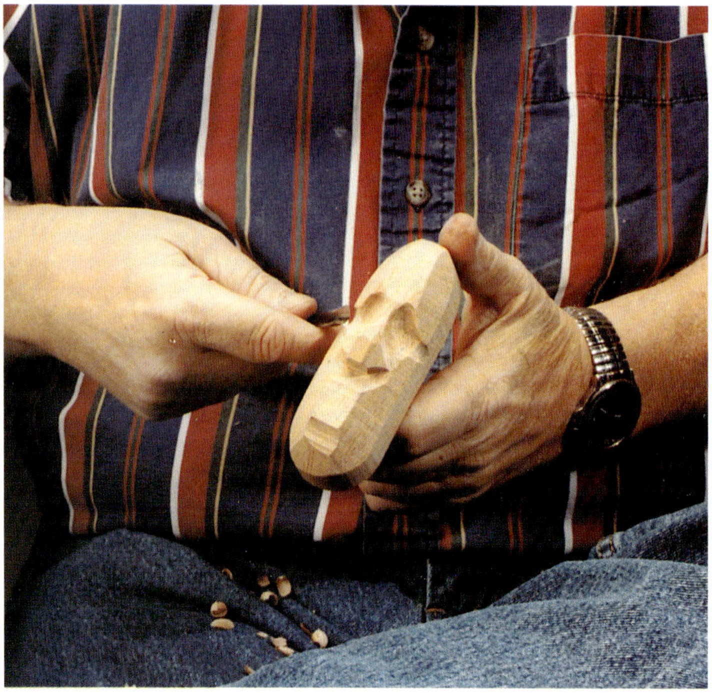

Progress. I'm using a Flexcut half round gouge to make these cuts.

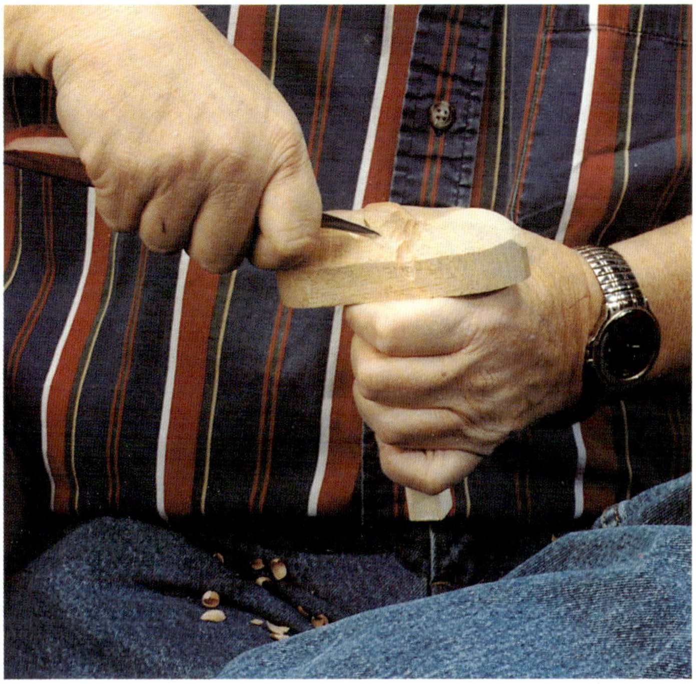

To accent the flange around the nostril, make three little cuts to form a triangle. Begin with a cut straight alongside the nose...

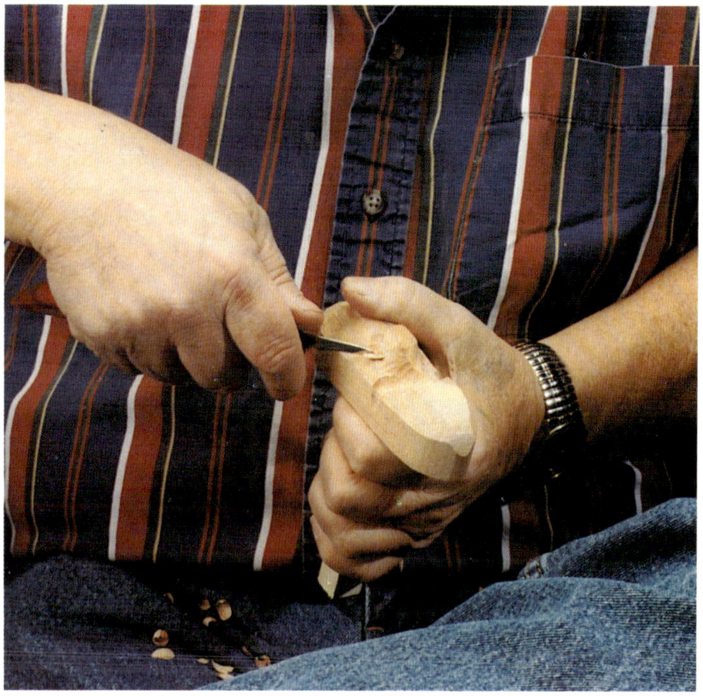

...then one up from the mouth.

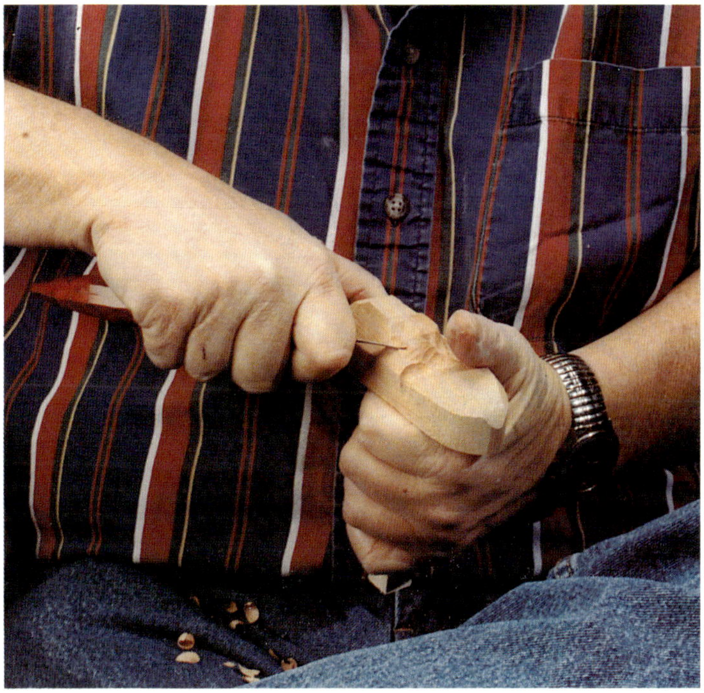

...then one from the cheekline,

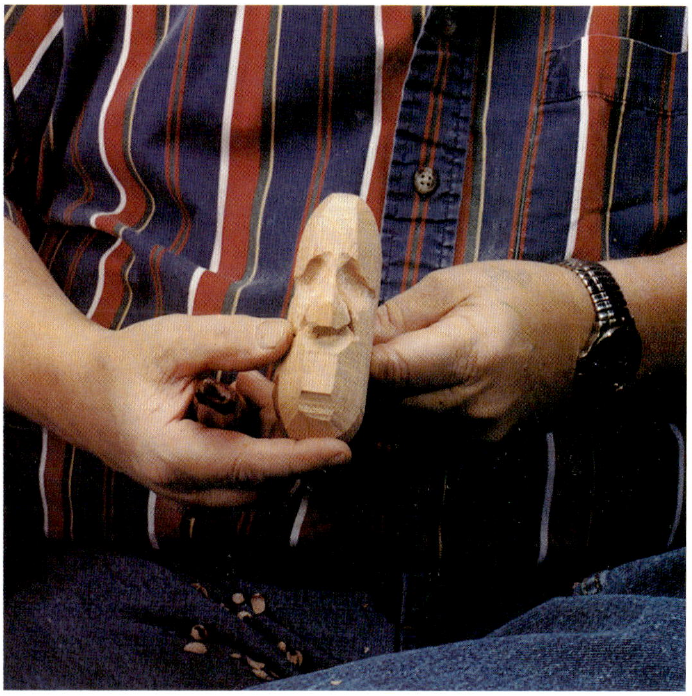

Progress. Don't bring this mark down too far yet, because you want to leave your options open for a moustache, beard, or dramatic facial expression.

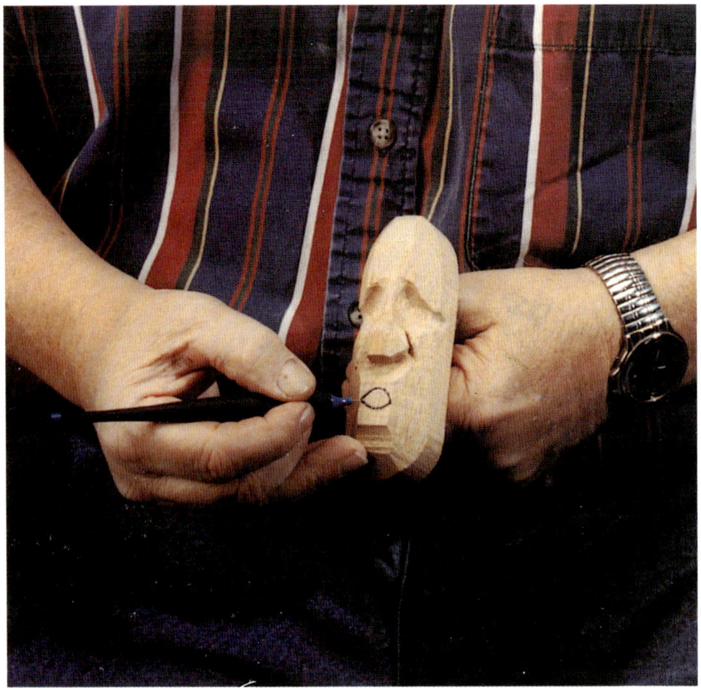

Maybe I'll give him a surprised look. I've marked the mouth with pen, for the camera's sake, but it's much better to use pencil.

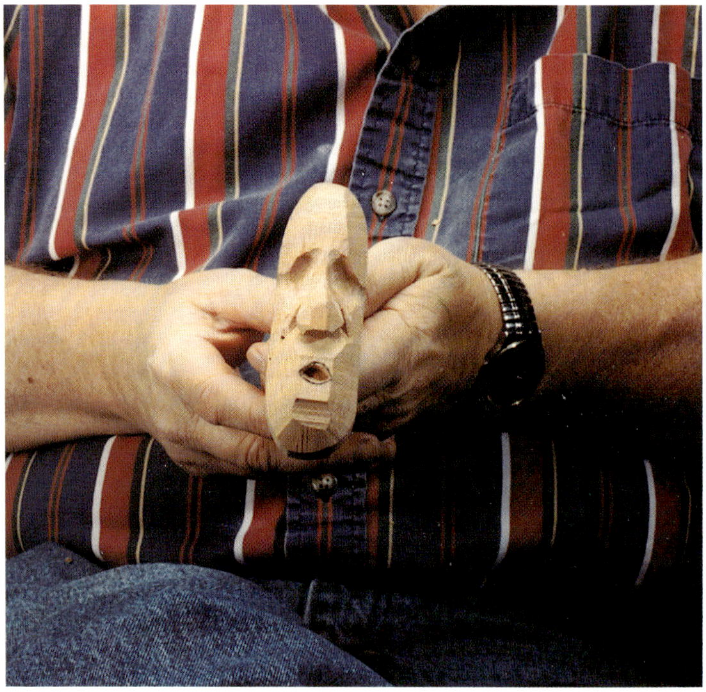

The deeper you cut, the more options you'll have with the lips.

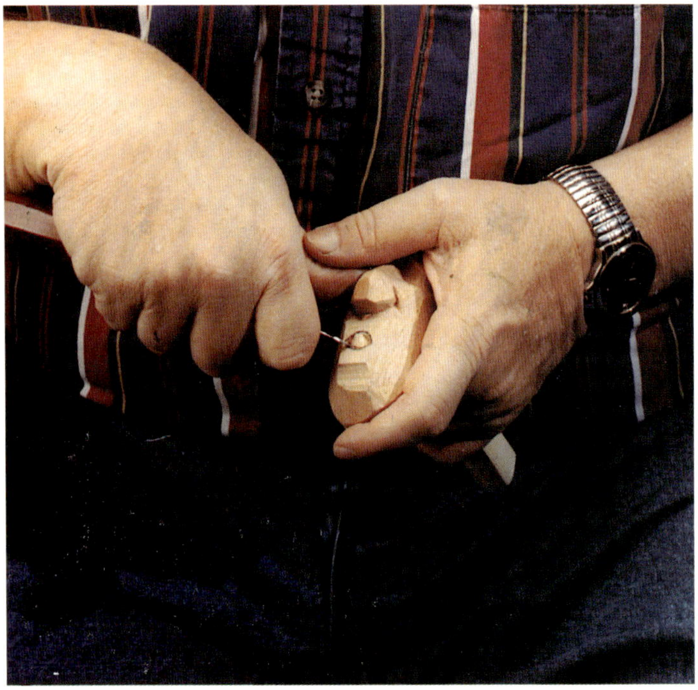

Cut in straight and deep around the mouth, and from the inside cut out to it.

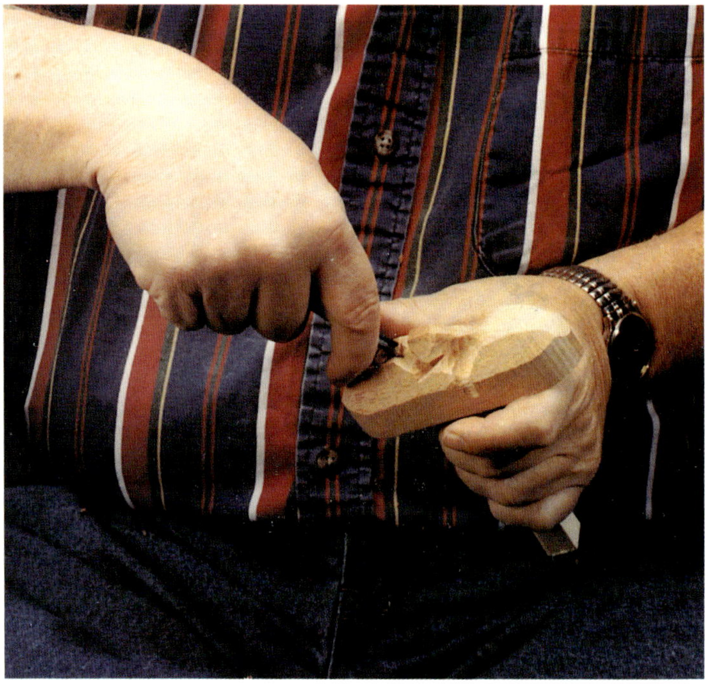

Use a half round gouge to make the philtrum, the indent under the nose.

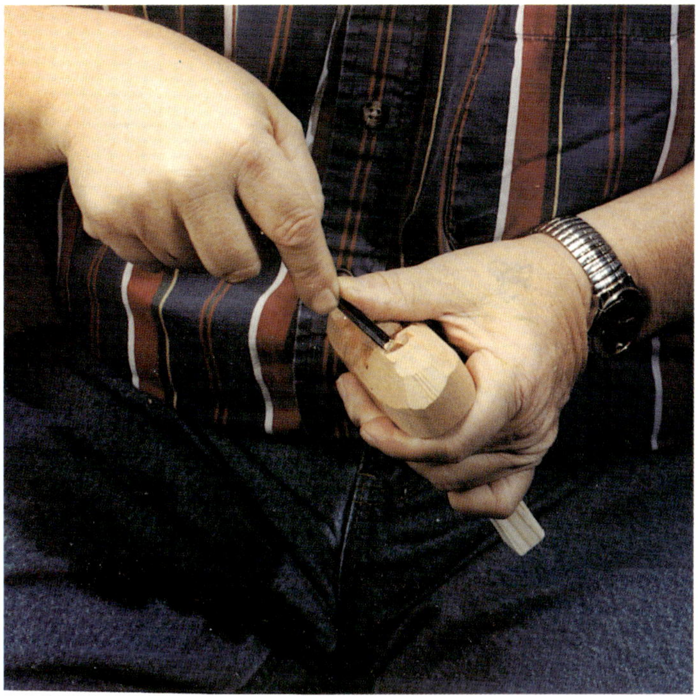

The lips have all kinds of muscles, which make them bulge in certain areas and decide their fullness. I'm separating the three areas on the upper lip.

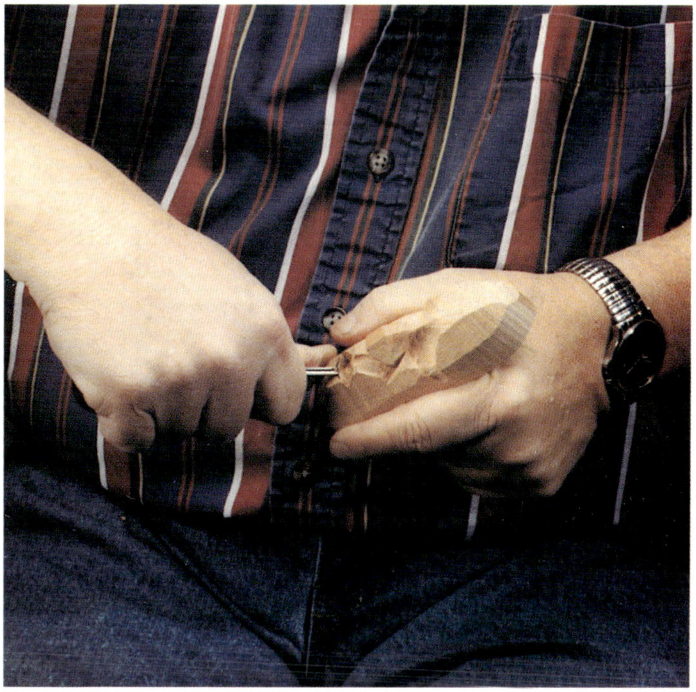

The lower lip needs a groove that I'll put in with this gouge.

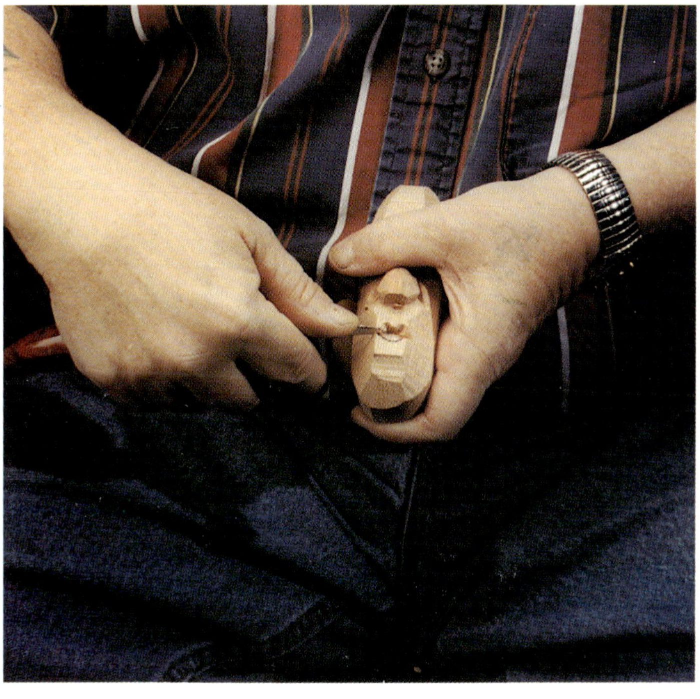

Bring out the corners of the mouth.

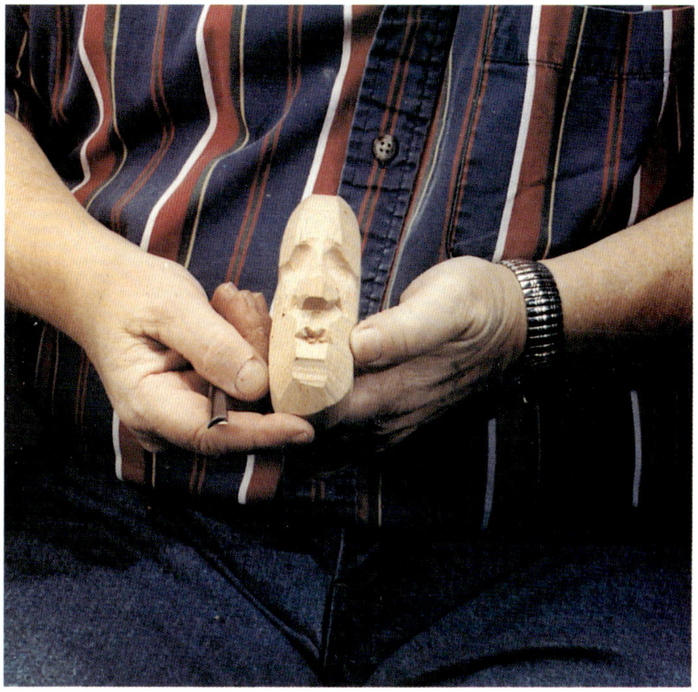

Here's the inside of the mouth before I start the outside.

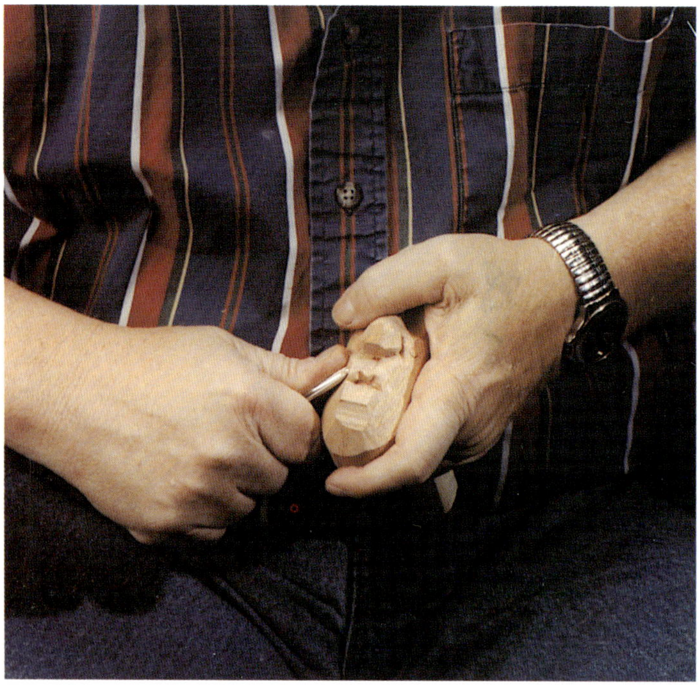

With the small half round I'm going along the outer edge of the upper lip to push the lip out more. Smooth it into the face.

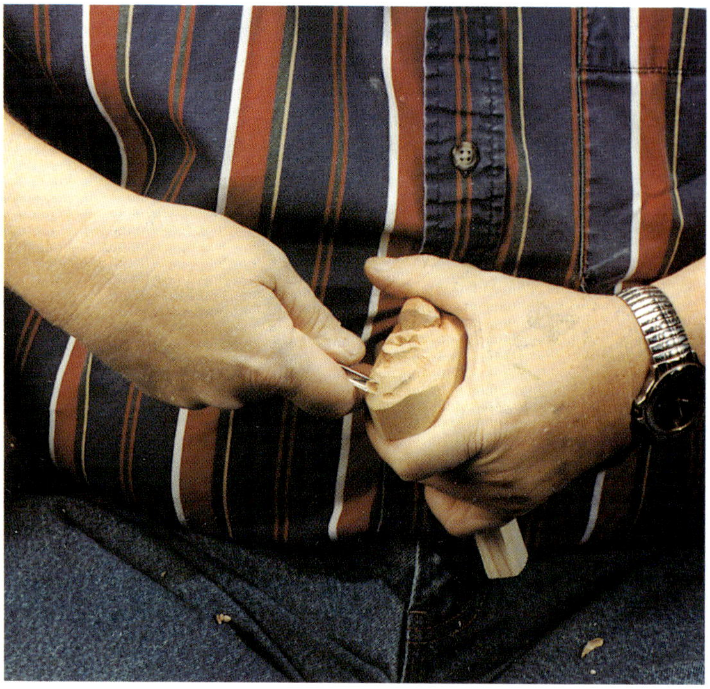

While I'm down here, I'll work down around the chin to bring it out.

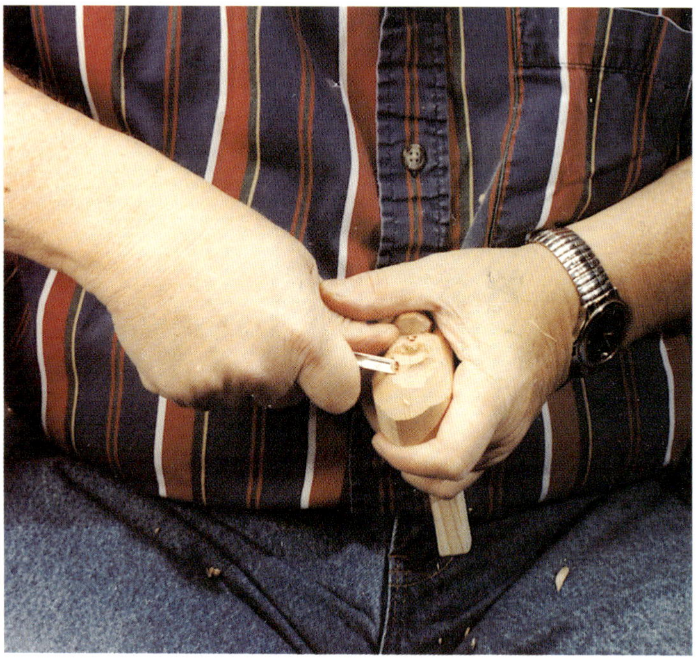

Under the lower lip I'm going deep to really make it curl over.

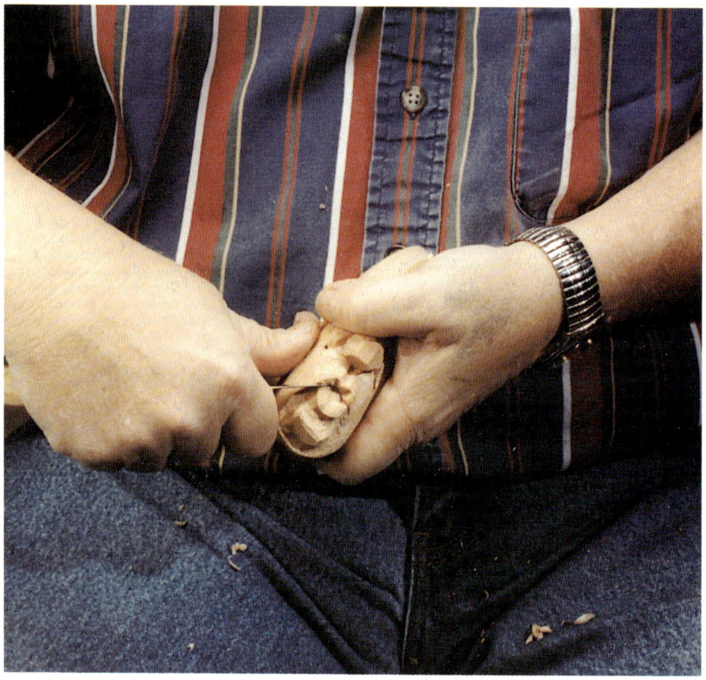

To bring the lower lip curling under the upper, Make a stop cut at the corner of the mouth and then cut up to it at an angle.

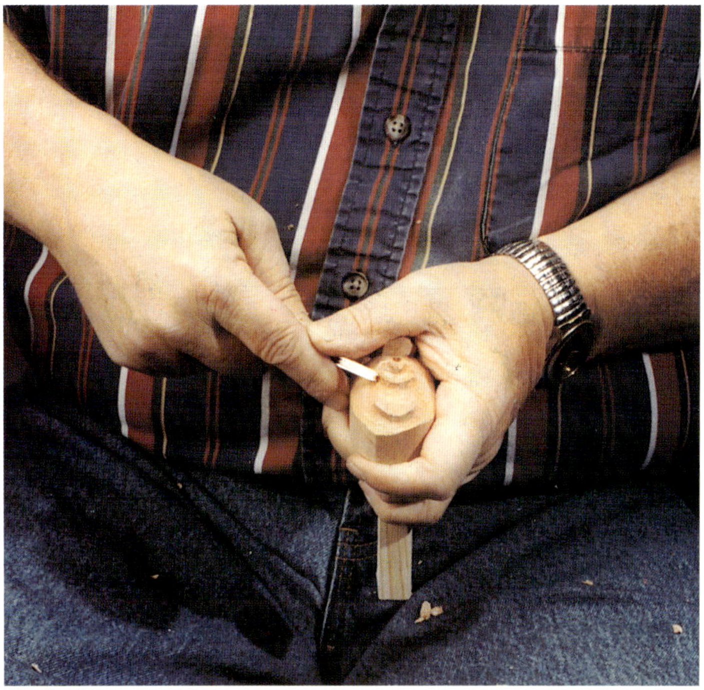

Take the veiner to the cut we just made and bring it under the lower lip to blend it.

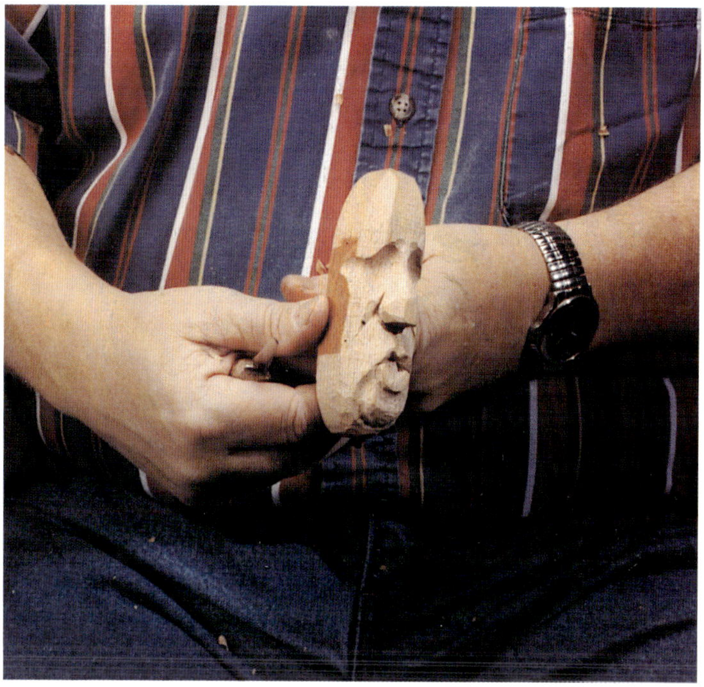

Progress.

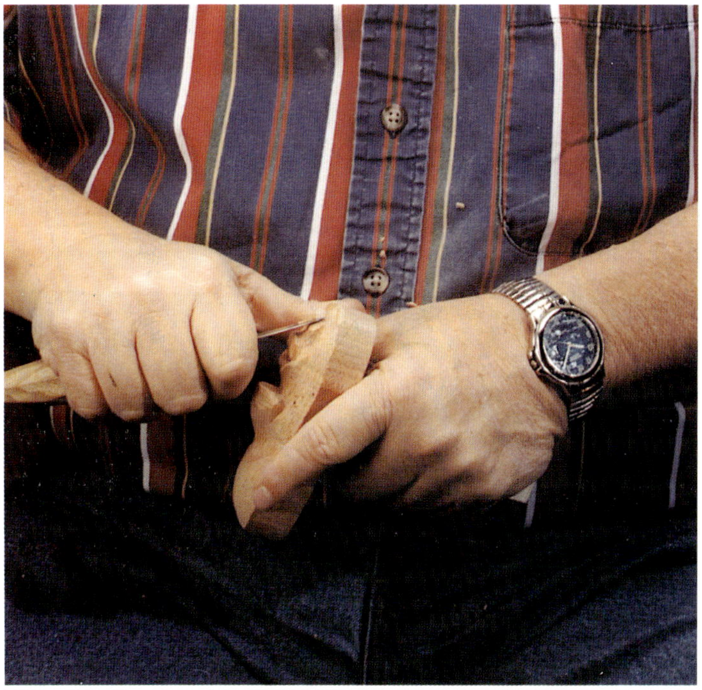

Refining the chin with a knife.

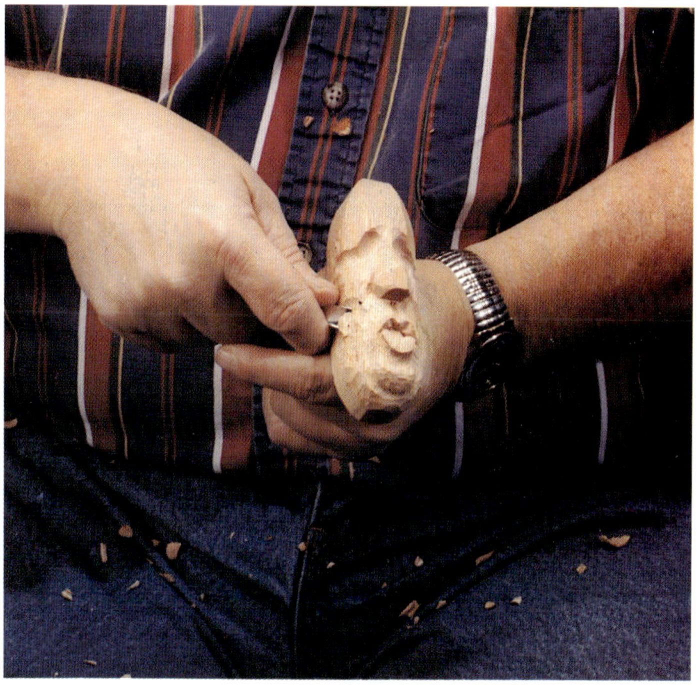

With a gouge, I'm sinking the cheeks in a little bit under the cheekbone.

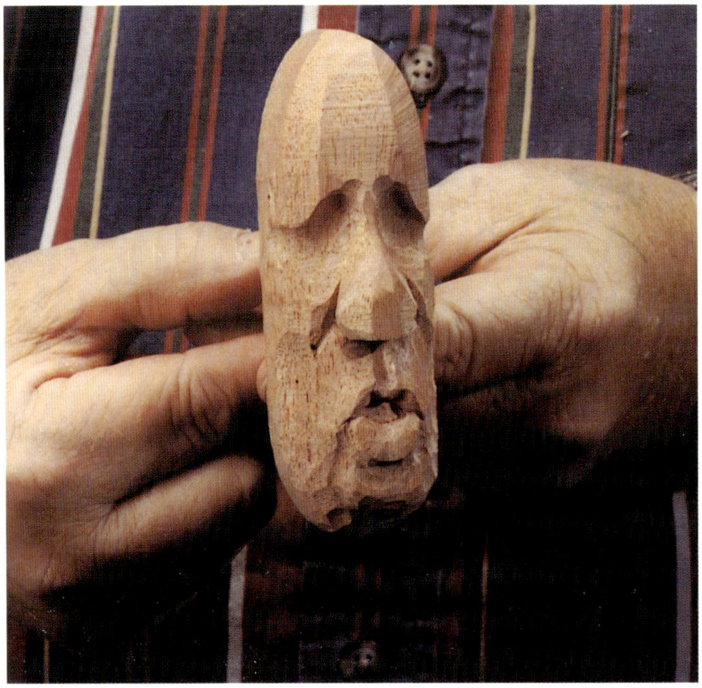

Progress.

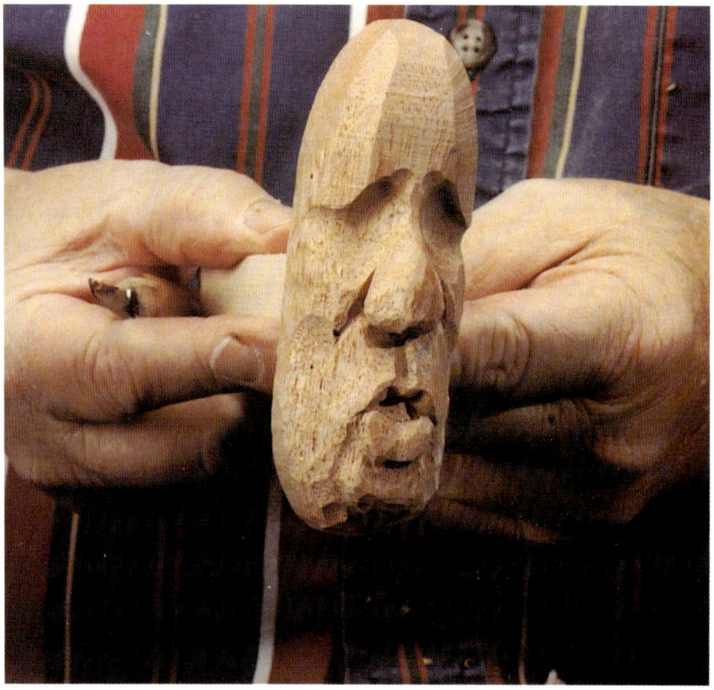

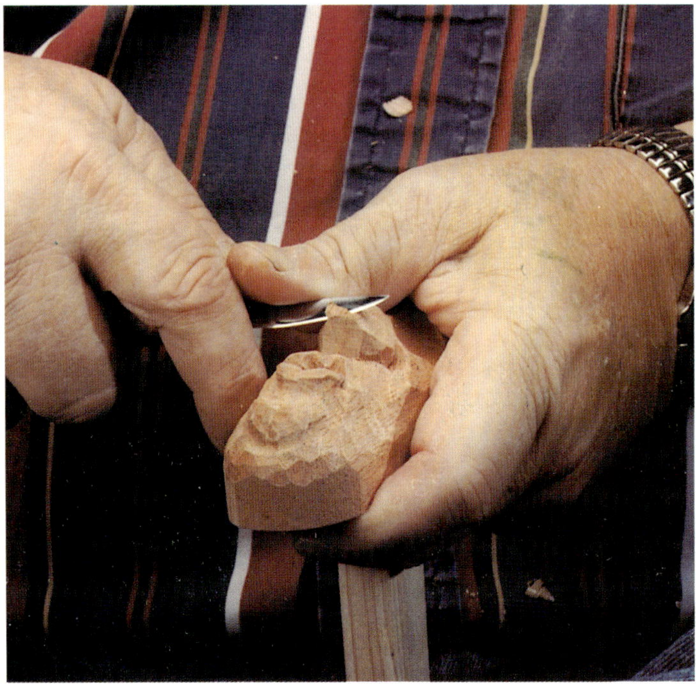

With a knife, I'm rounding off the corners on the nose.

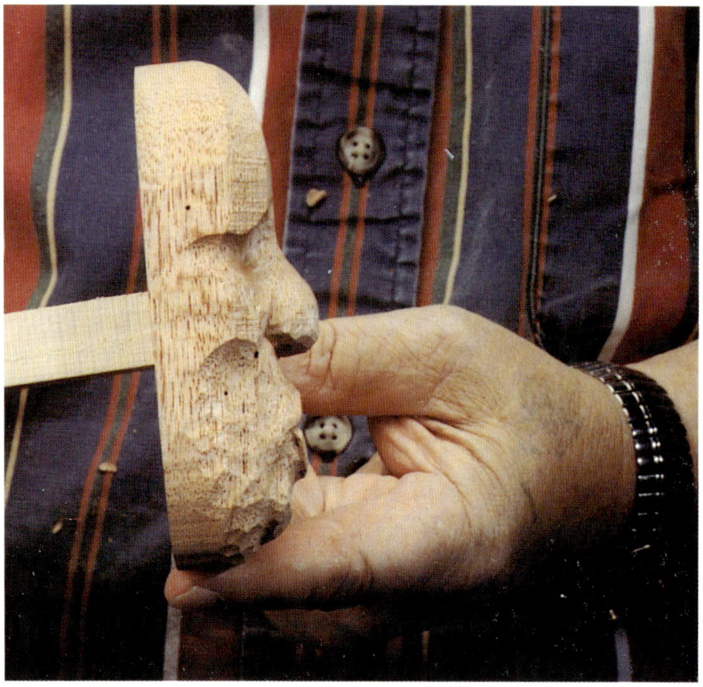

At this point, there's all kinds of things we can do with this nose.

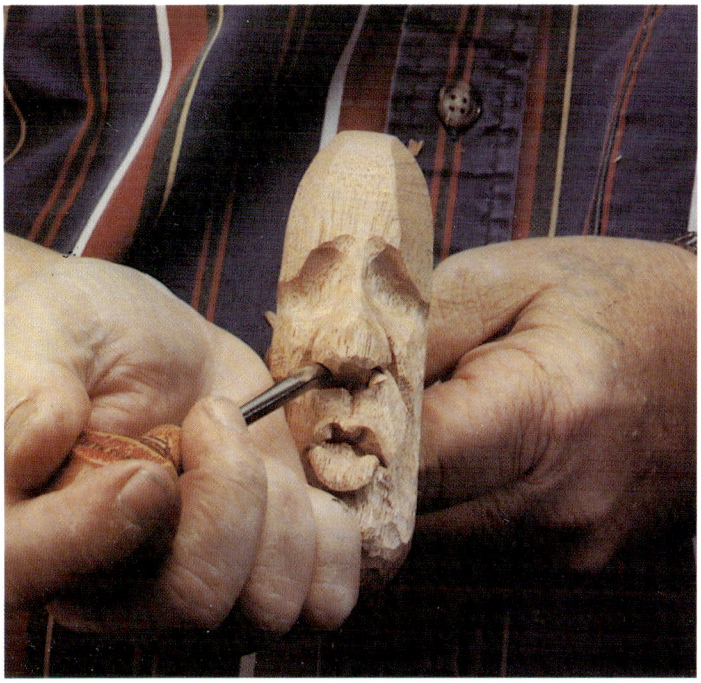

To make the nostrils, dig in with a gouge. My advice is to make the nostrils a little further apart than you might otherwise.

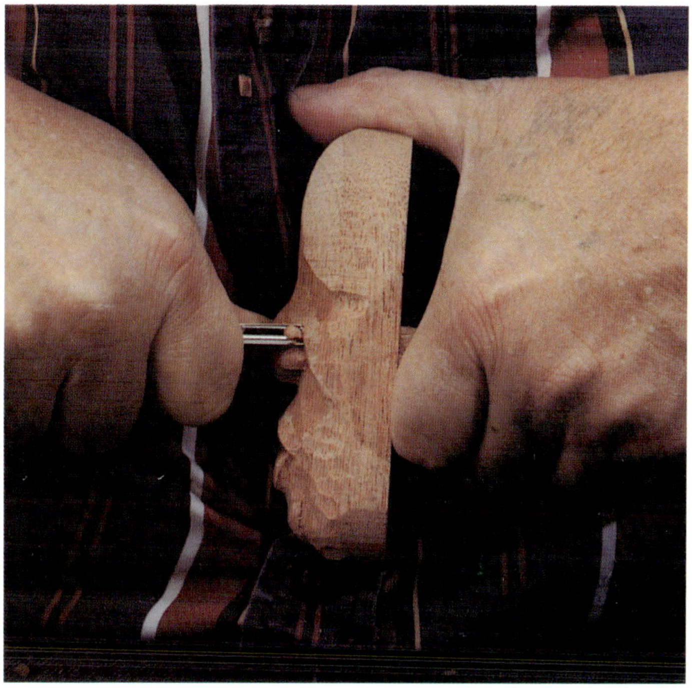

The half round is good for defining the nostril flange.

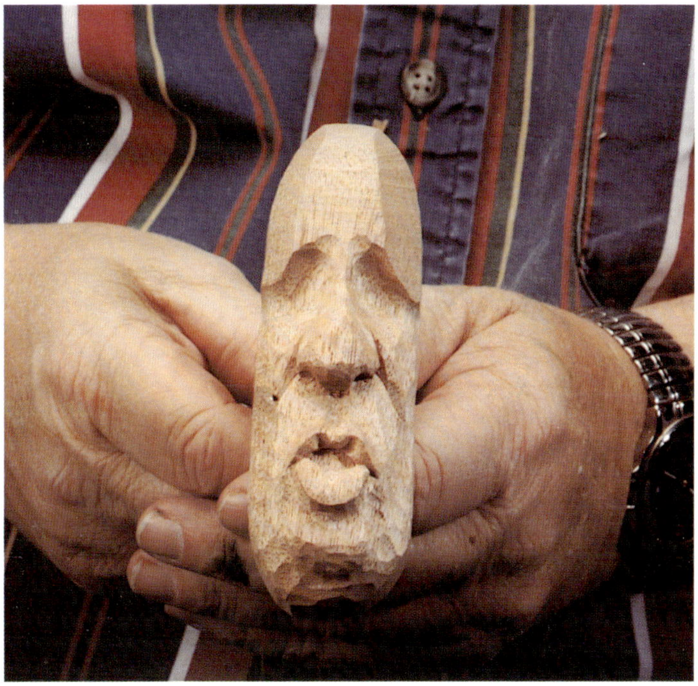

Progress.

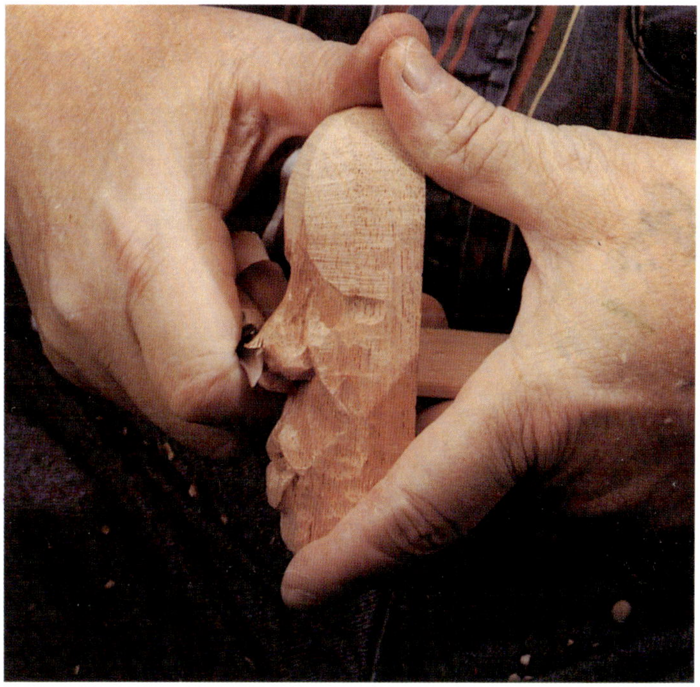

The nose looks too big to me. I'm going to change the profile.

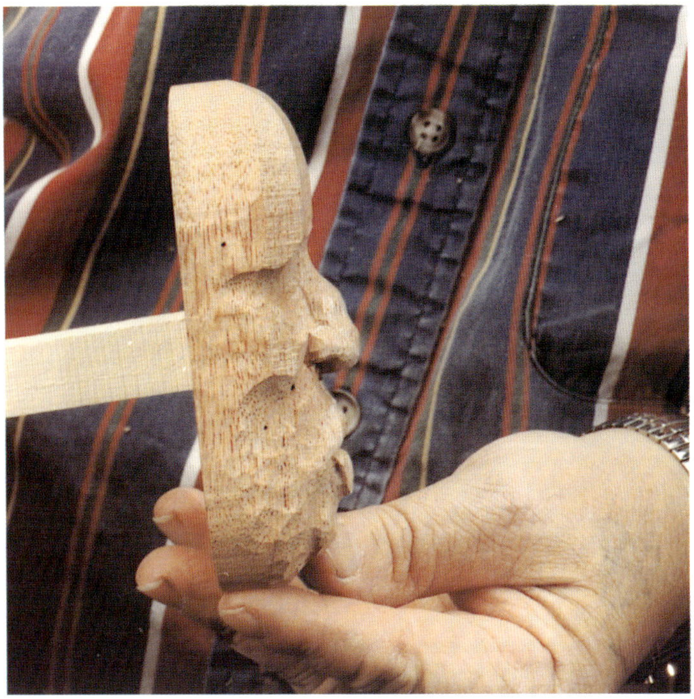

I think he's had a broken nose before.

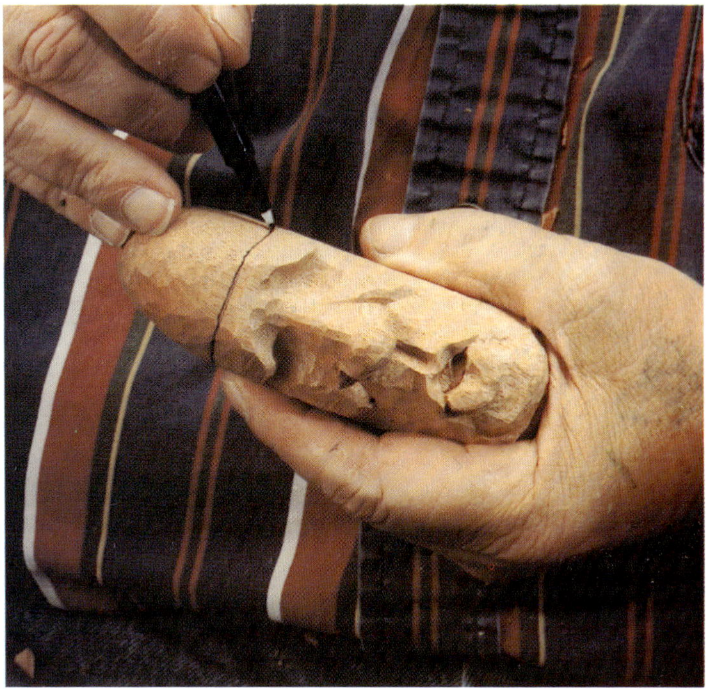

I think he needs a helmet. It might be to ride a Harley or to ride a Dragonship, I haven't decided.

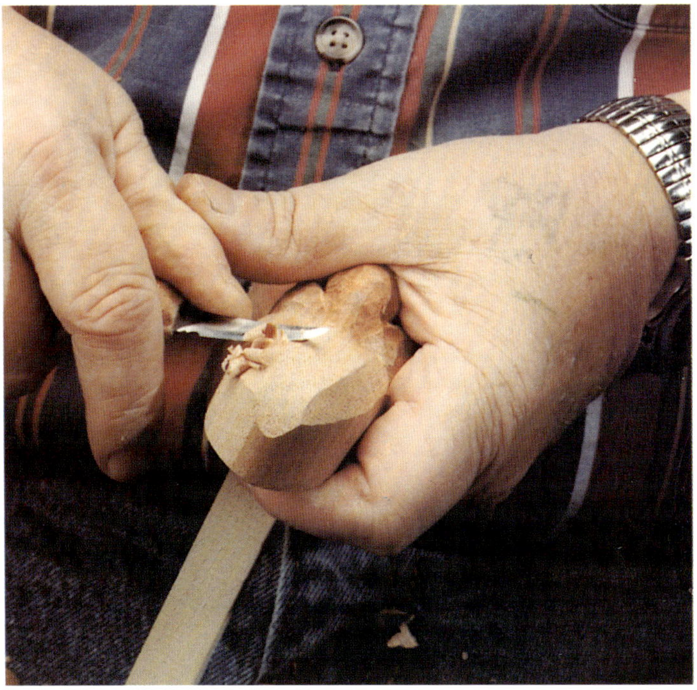

Now I'm rounding off the top of the head.

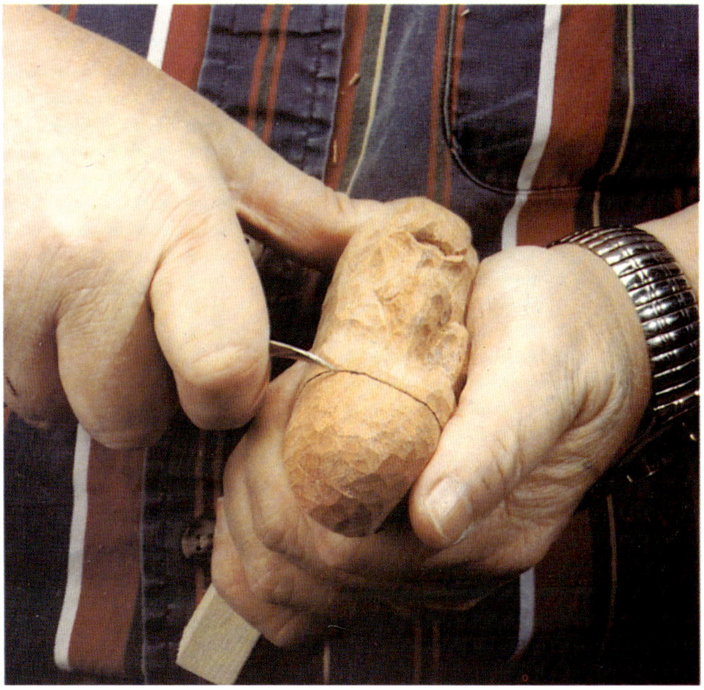

I'm making a stop cut where I've marked.

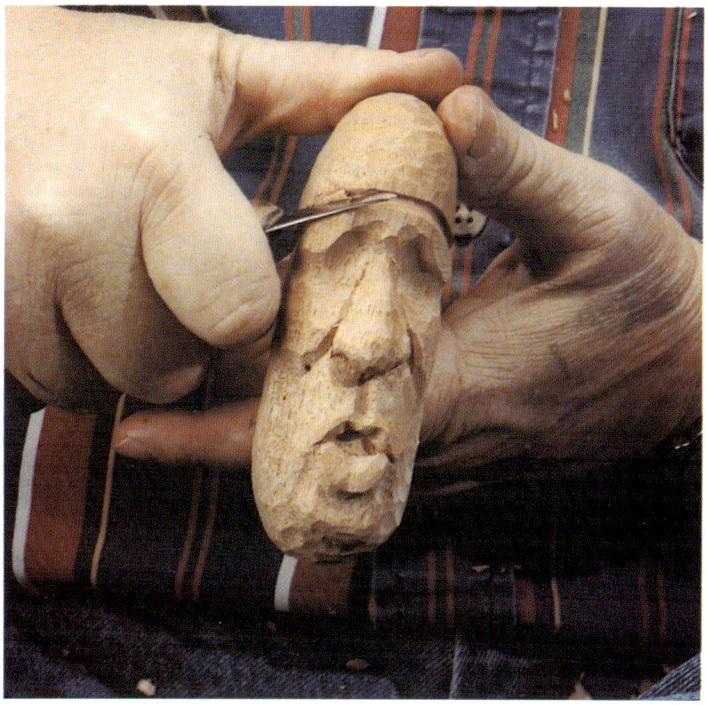

Cut up to it from thc forehead.

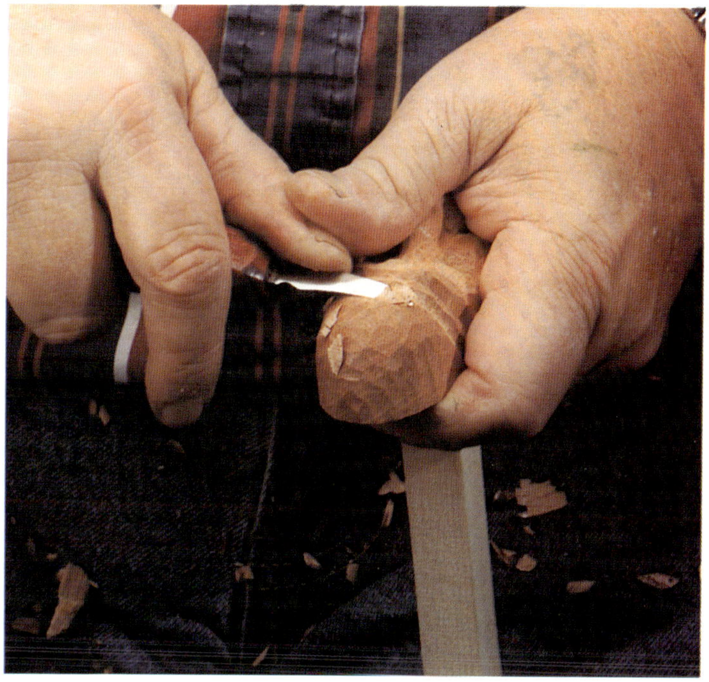

Just like the upper lip, smooth the new groove up into the helmet.

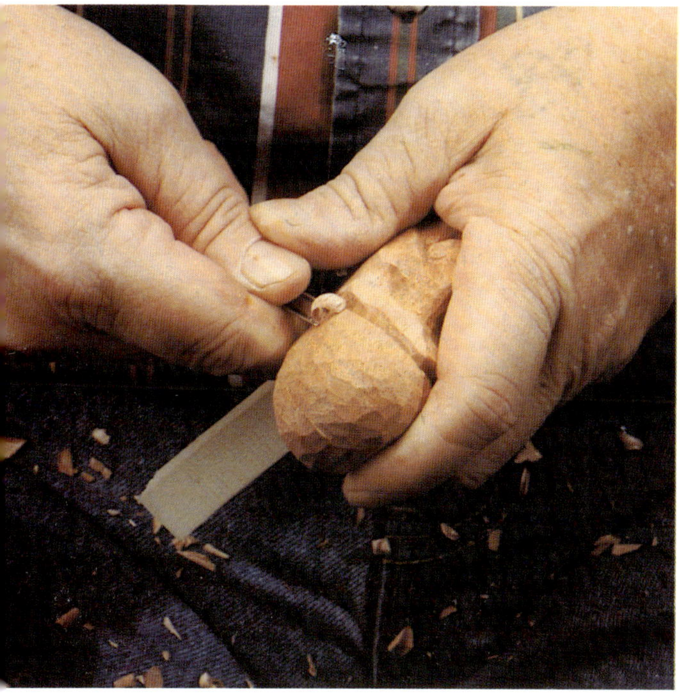

Bring out the edge of the helmet by cutting above the helmet with a small half round.

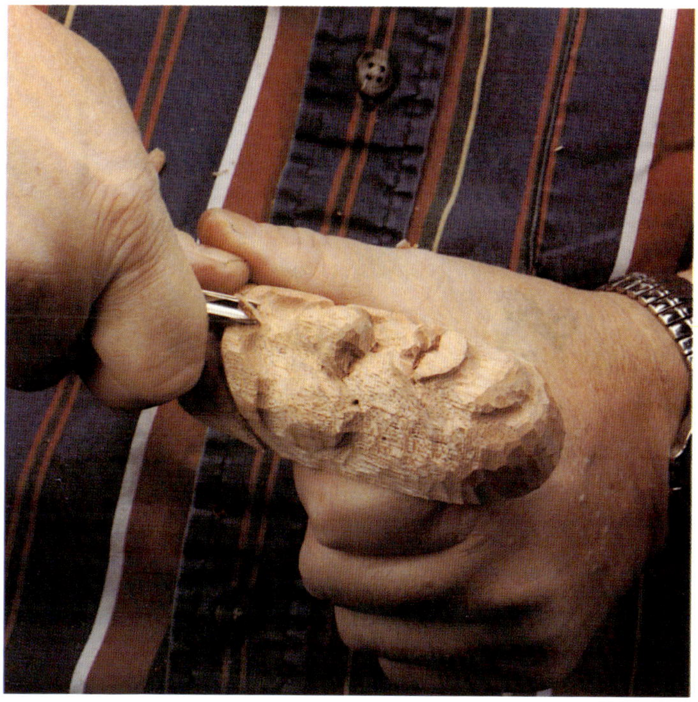

Nip a little out from between the eyebrows to make them stand out better.

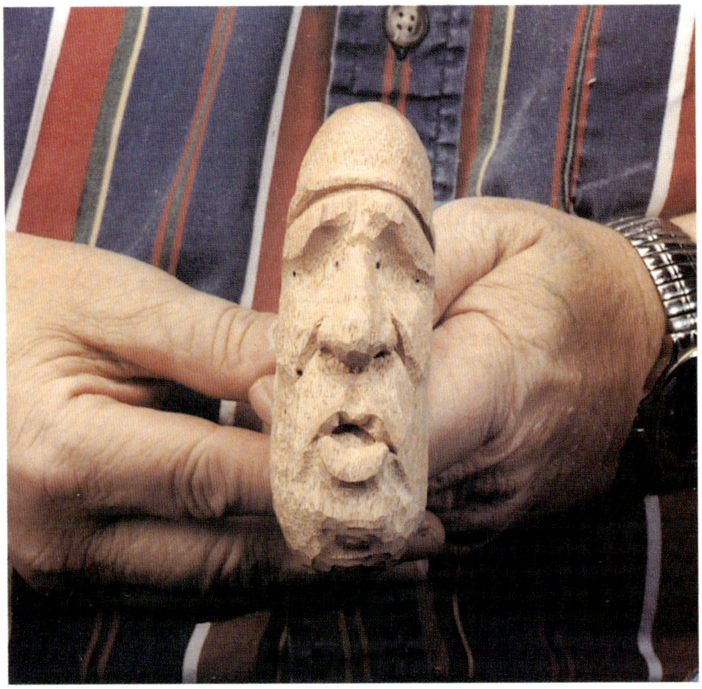

When you're deciding the eye position, remember that realistically the distance between the two tear ducts (across the bridge of the nose) is equal to the length of the eye itself.

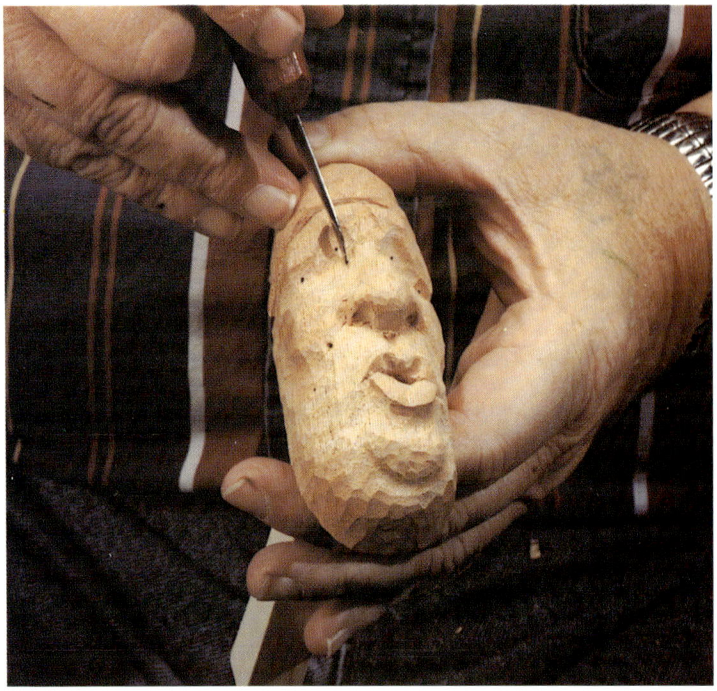

I've drawn three points for each eye that give us the general shape. Now we'll make some cuts into each one.

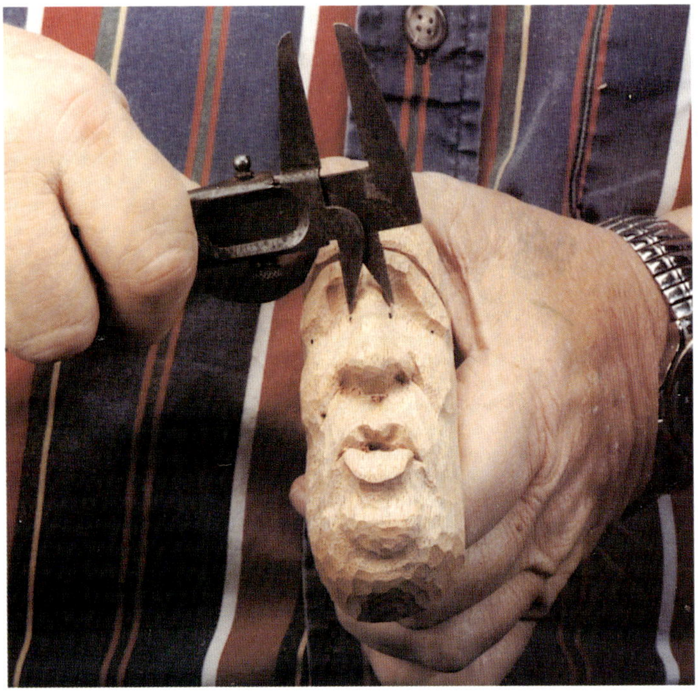

In case you're trying to break that nasty bird-carving habit and have one of these tools laying around, they're helpful for measuring. I found mine at a flea market and I just figured out what it's for.

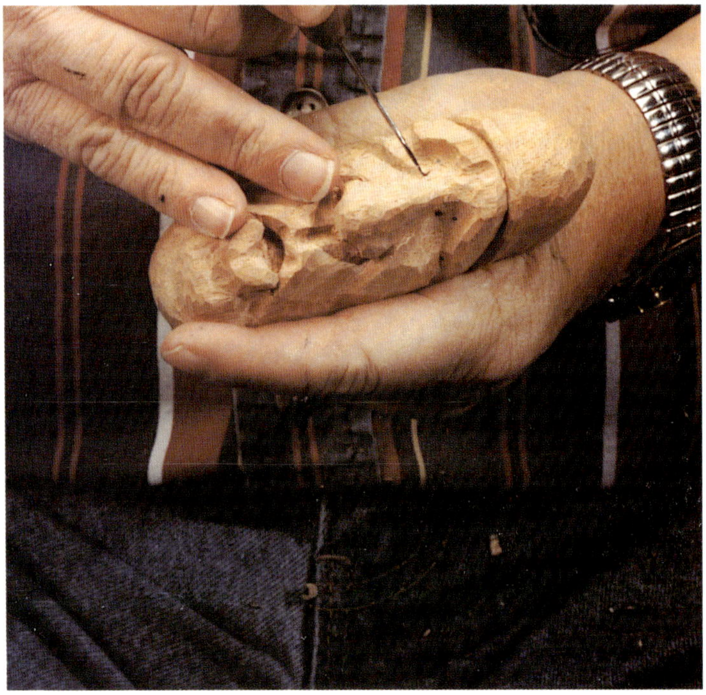

For each point you want three cuts, very similar to the ones we made around the nostrils.

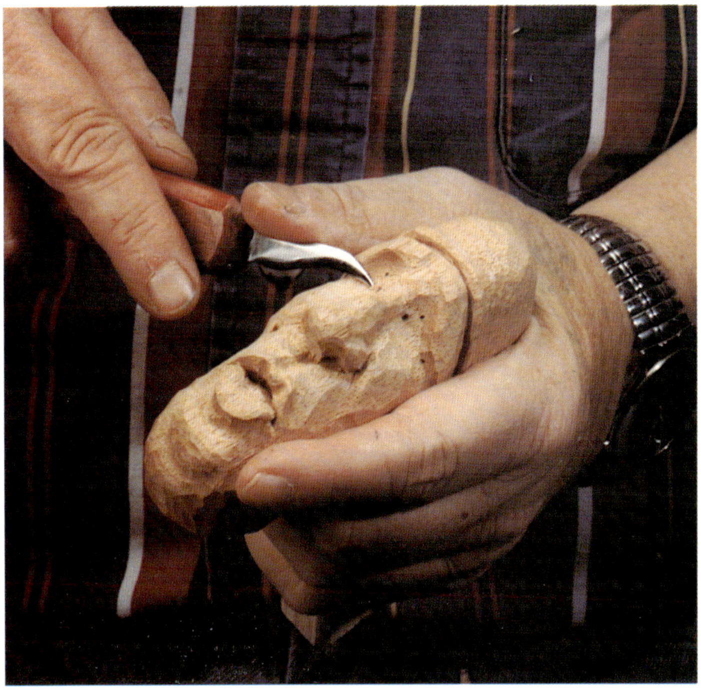

Make sure each of these little triangles frames the eyeball-to-be.

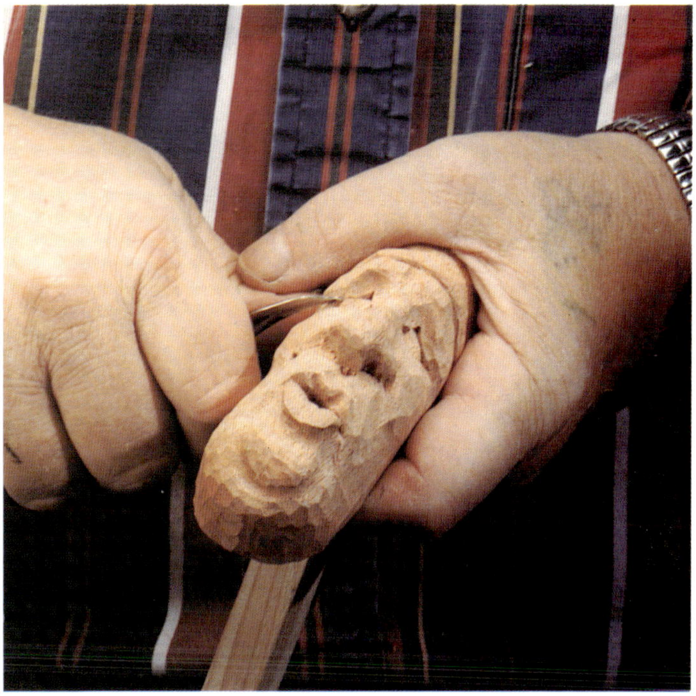

Now we'll connect each cut with a stop cut.

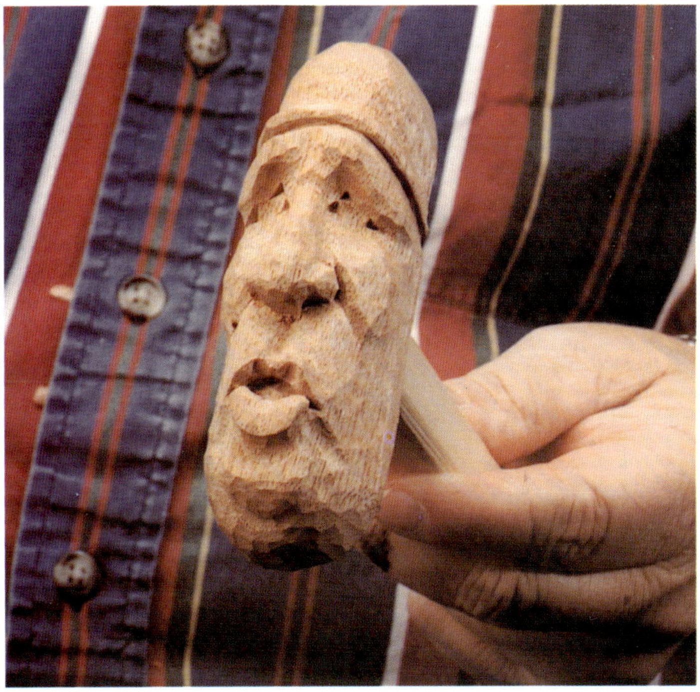

Progress.

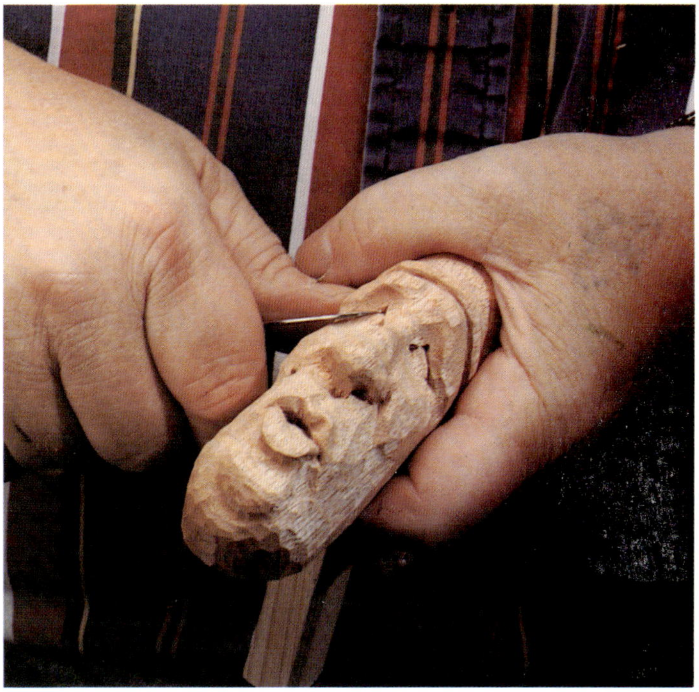

Come at the cut from the eye at a sharp angle.

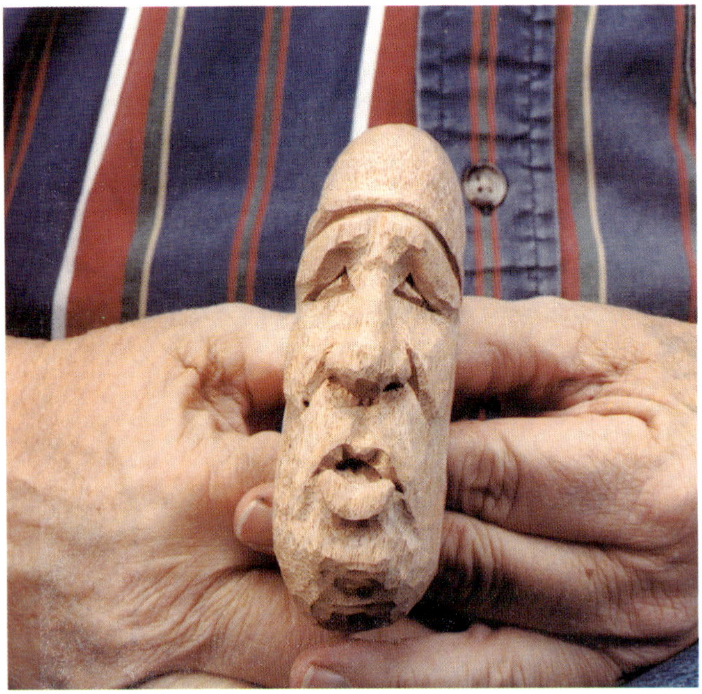

Progress.

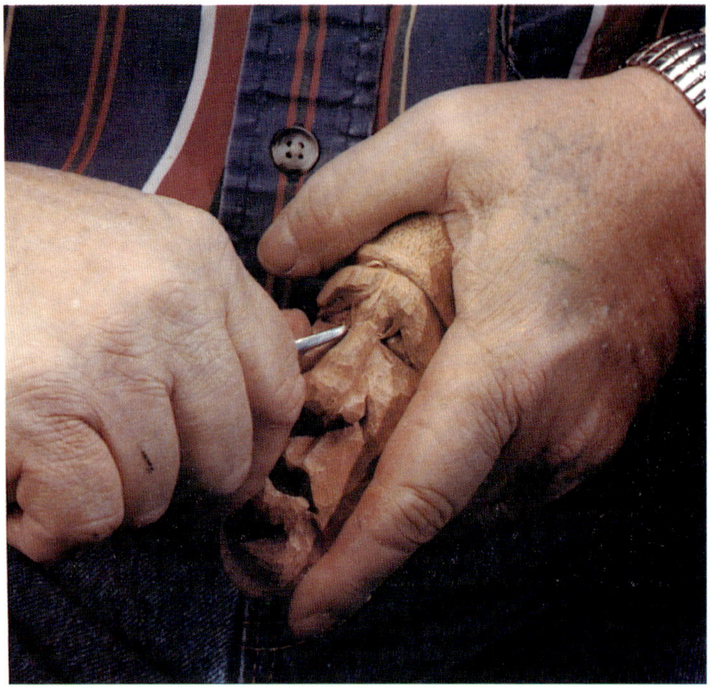

For an underlid, cut up into the tear duct and finish it with a curve. Don't pass the duct.

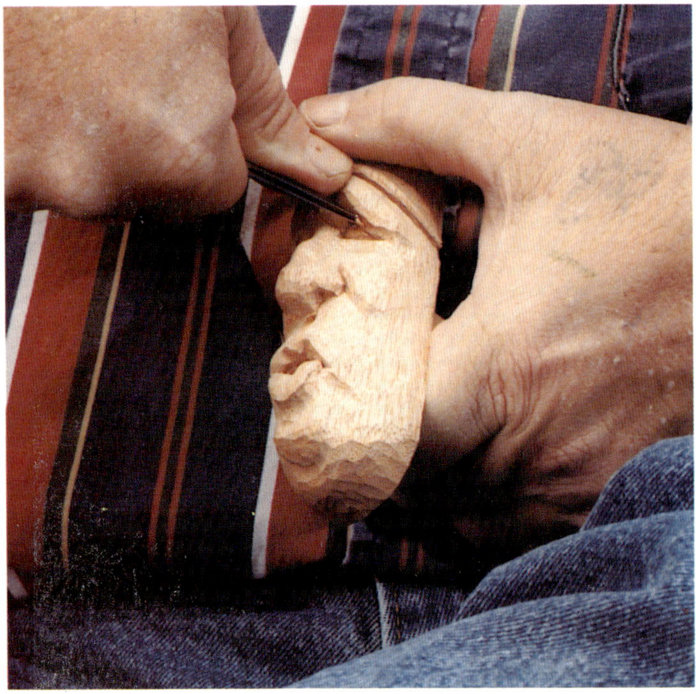

I use a veiner for the eyelids. The trick is to get as close to the eye as you can without breaking its line.

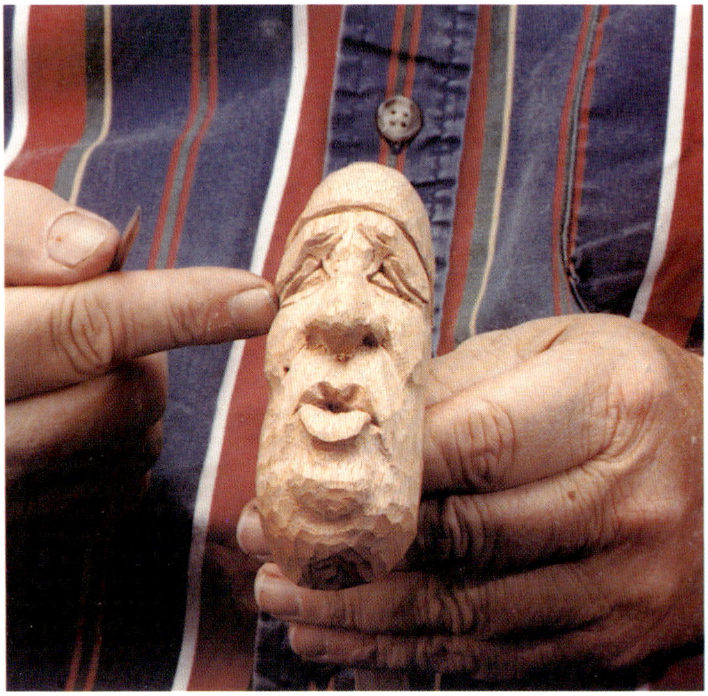

There's too much angle in the eyeballs, causing too many shadows. I'm going to smooth it out some.

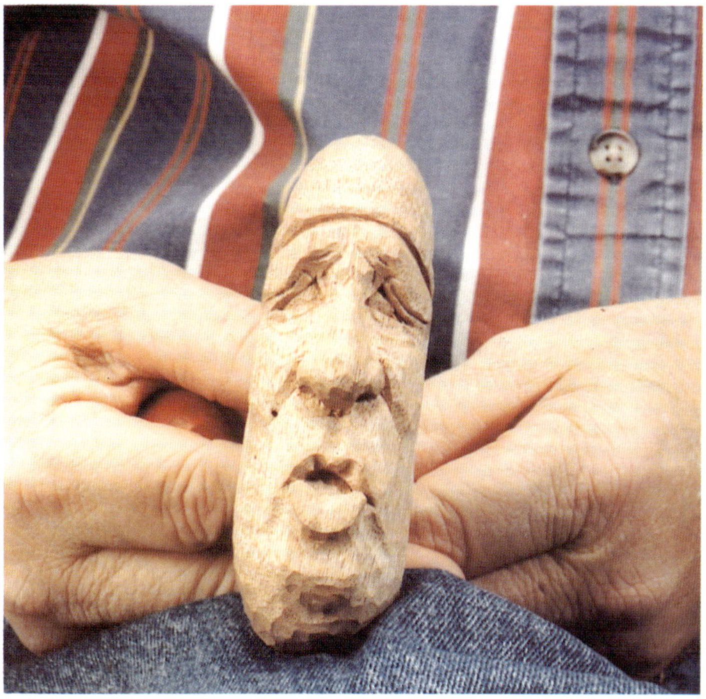

I used a small flat gouge for the job.

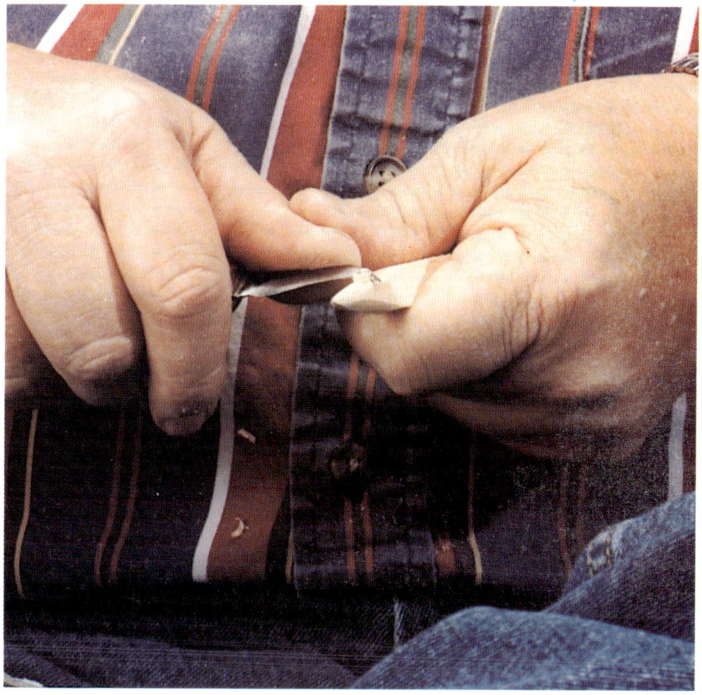

I'm making some horns for the helmet from a scrap piece of basswood for a nice contrast with the mahogany.

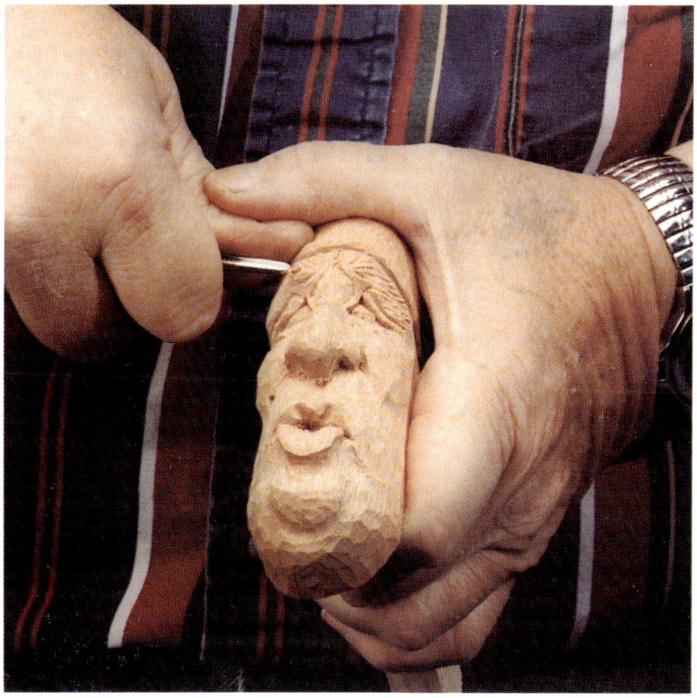

Big, bushy eyebrows. I like to use a veiner to do this.

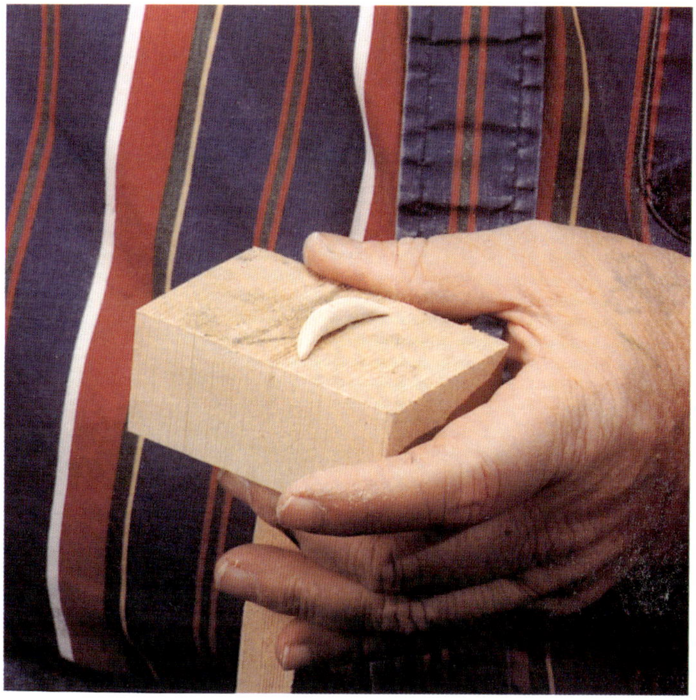

It's easier to start out with just one piece; hold on to one end while you carve the other.

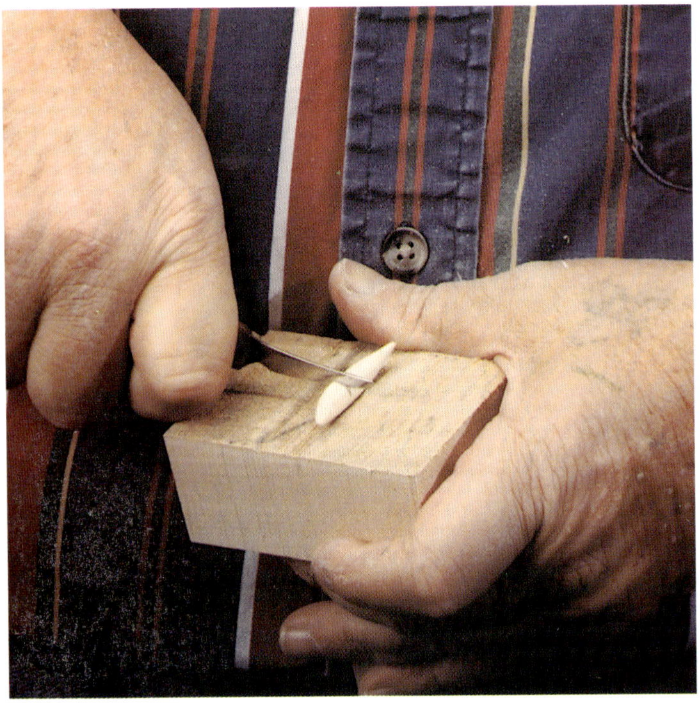

Then cut it in half when you're done.

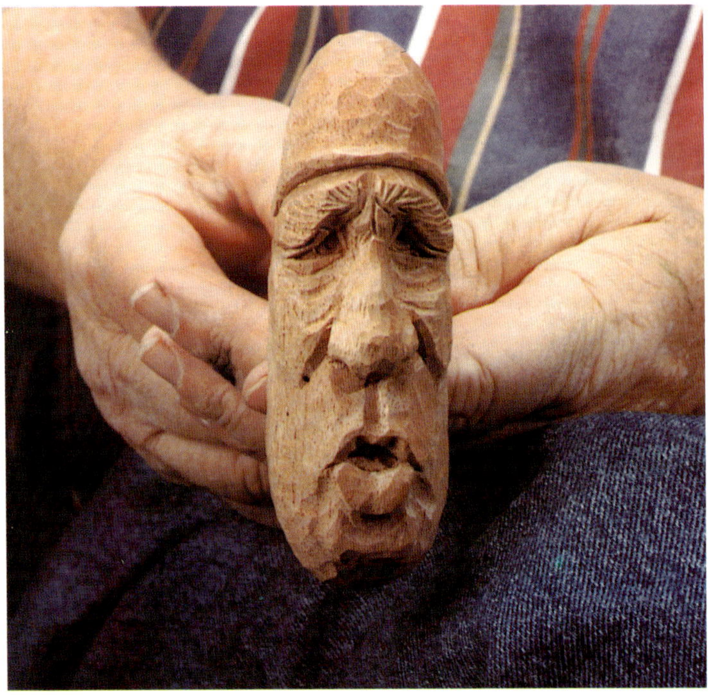

A smaller punch makes the pupil.

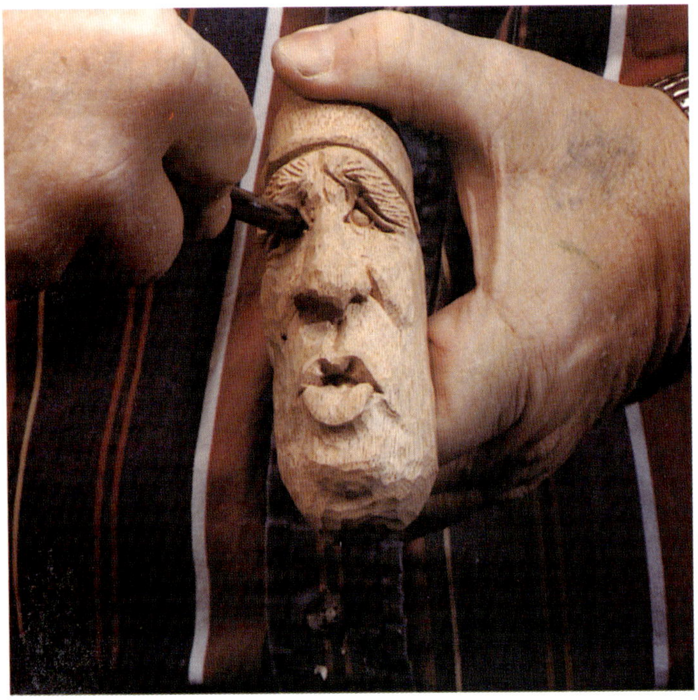

I use an eyepunch to make the iris of the eye.

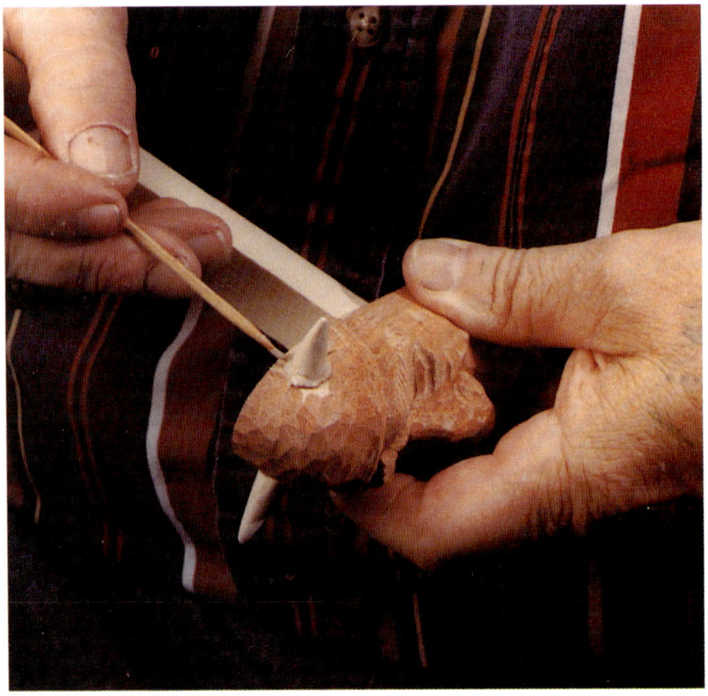

I'm using two different glues to put the horns on. I put super glue on one side, and regular wood glue on the other. I'm lumping some wood glue where the pieces meet. If it gets messy, you can sand the extra off with paper or a rotary tool.

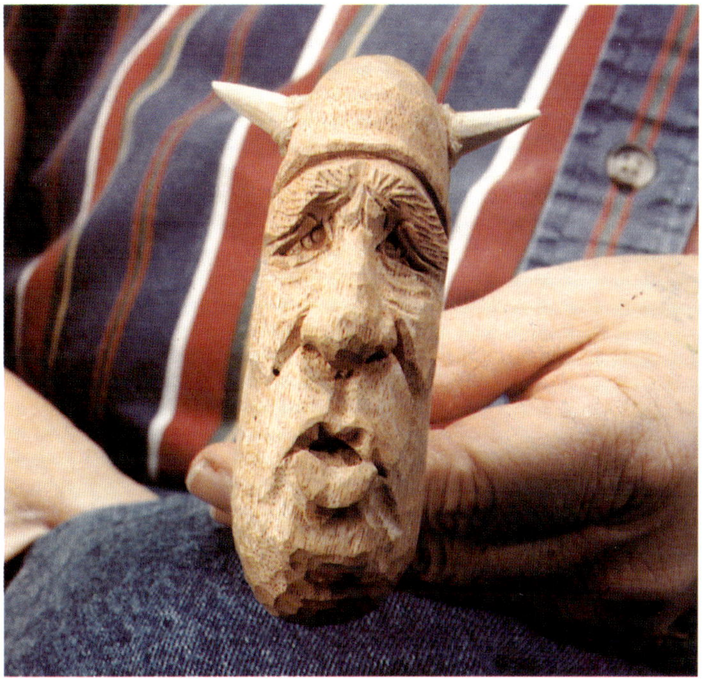

The finished viking.

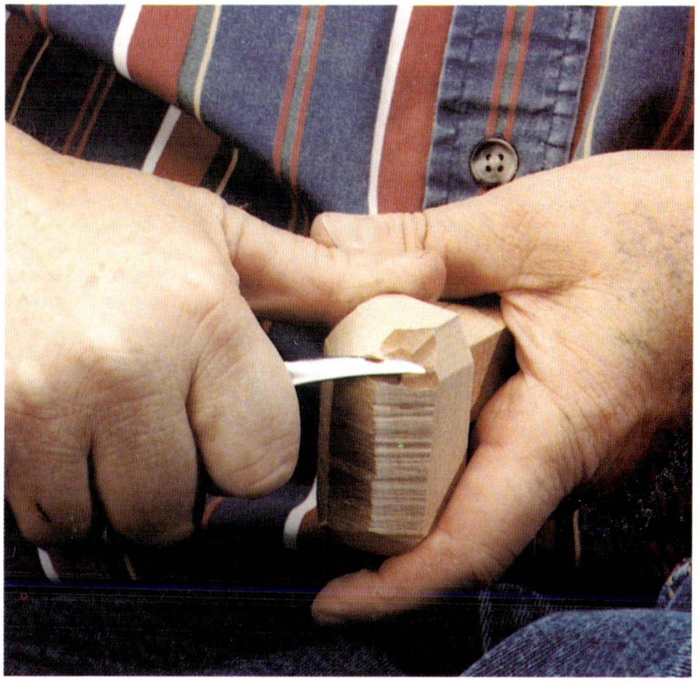

By now, our first piece has had enough time to dry, so we're ready to carve. I'm rounding the corners and edges, making sure the face is balanced.

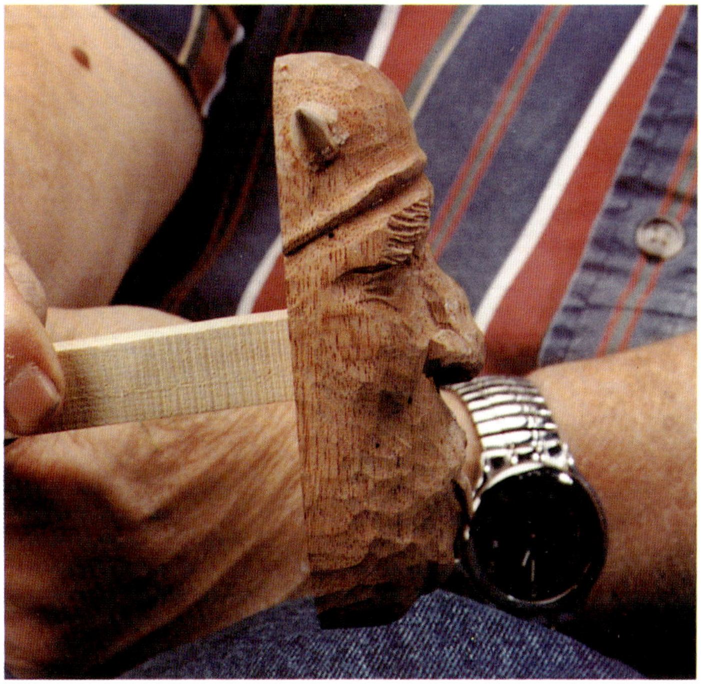

Profile. The handle will stay on until I need to saw part or all of it off. A screw eye in the top of the head (and a length of string or ribbon) finishes your bottle spirit!

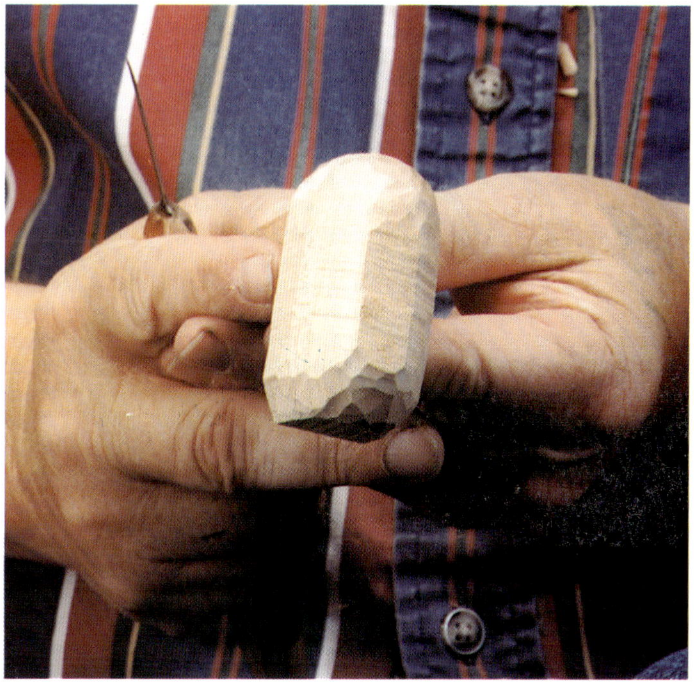

Progress.

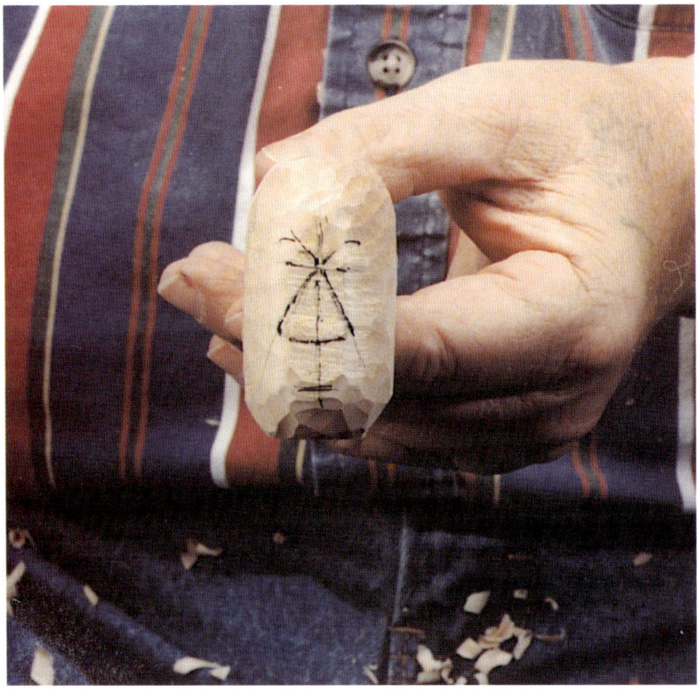

Make a center mark for the head, with an eye line intersecting it. Then mark a large, wide triangle for the nose.

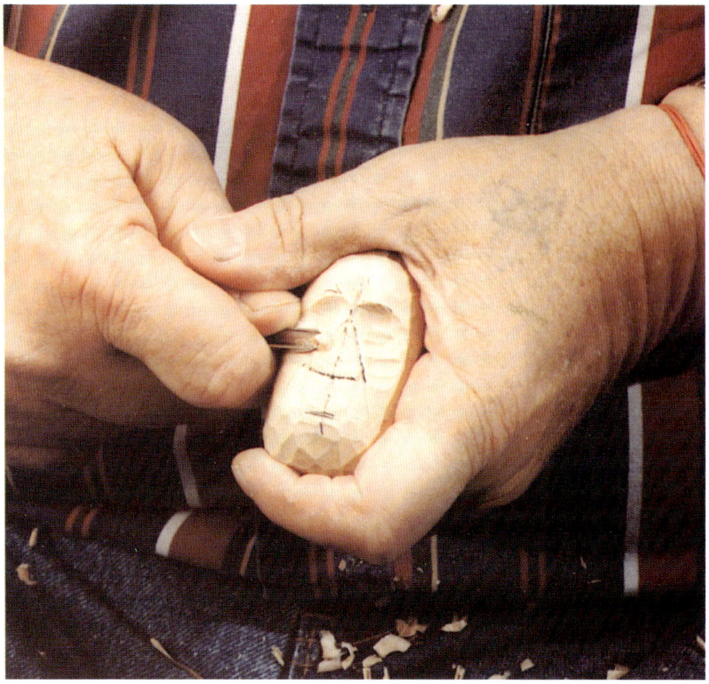

Progress.

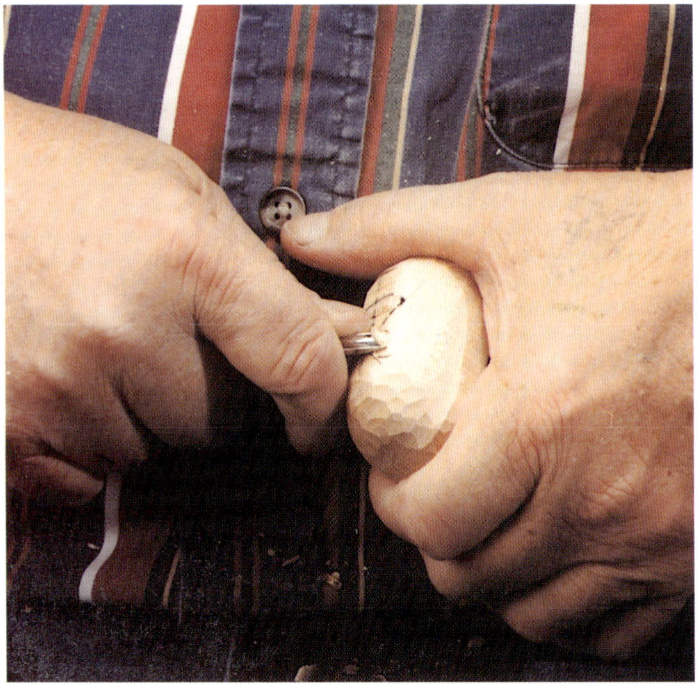

Start to bring the nose out under the eye with the gouge; start almost from the center line.

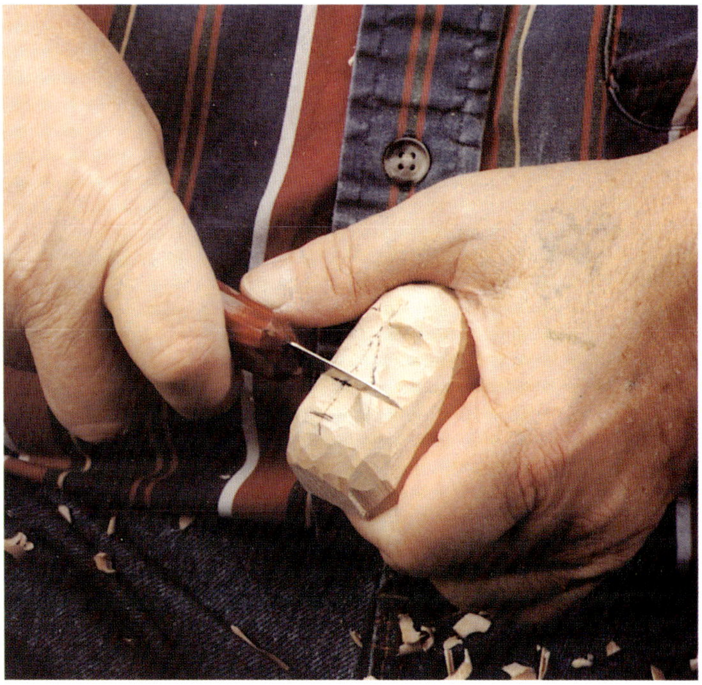

Make a stop cut straight across the bottom of the nose.

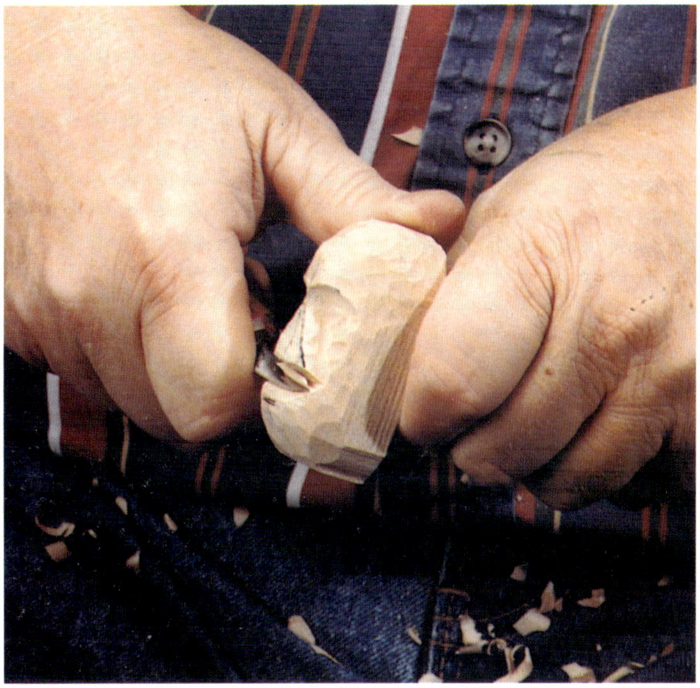

Cut up to it from where the mouth will be.

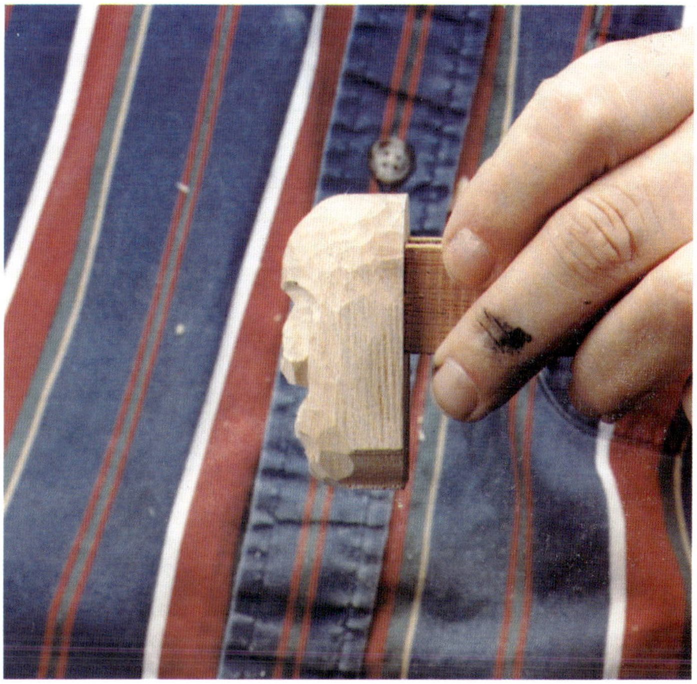

Profile.

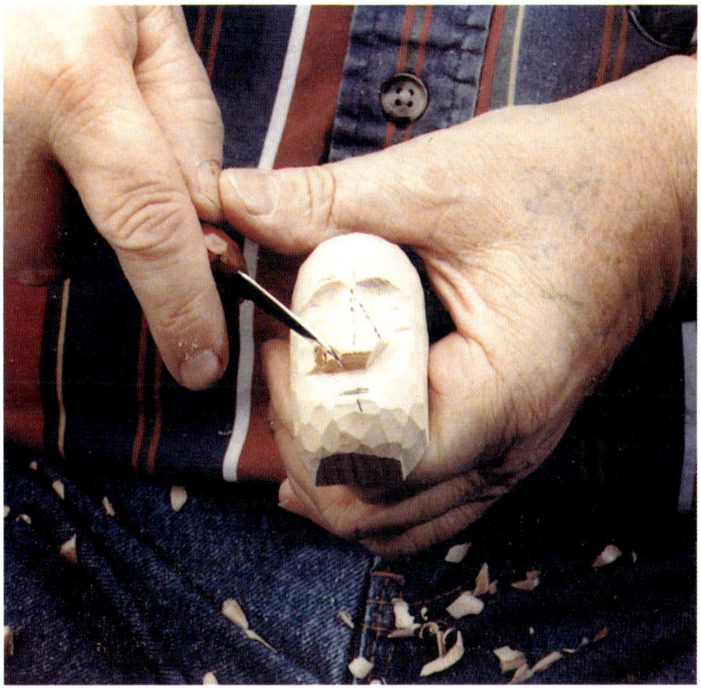

Nip off the corners where the nostrils will be.

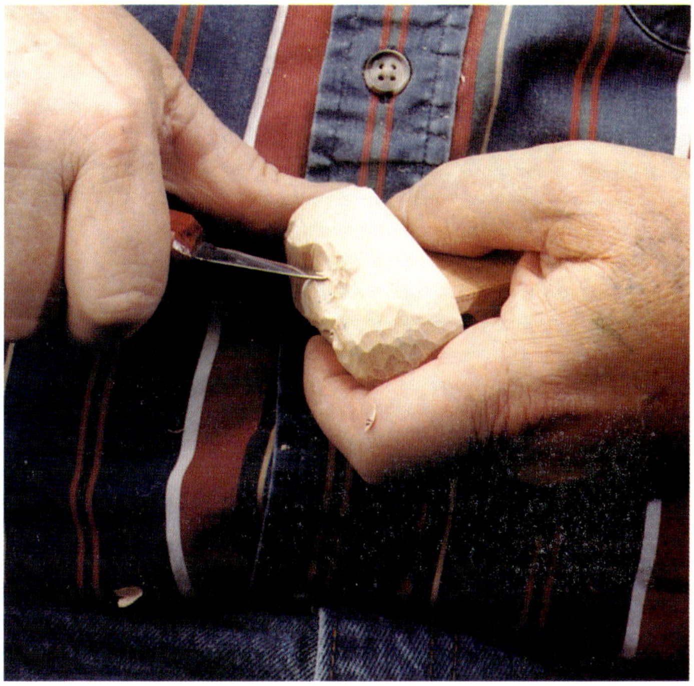

Make a stop cut straight down next to the nostril.

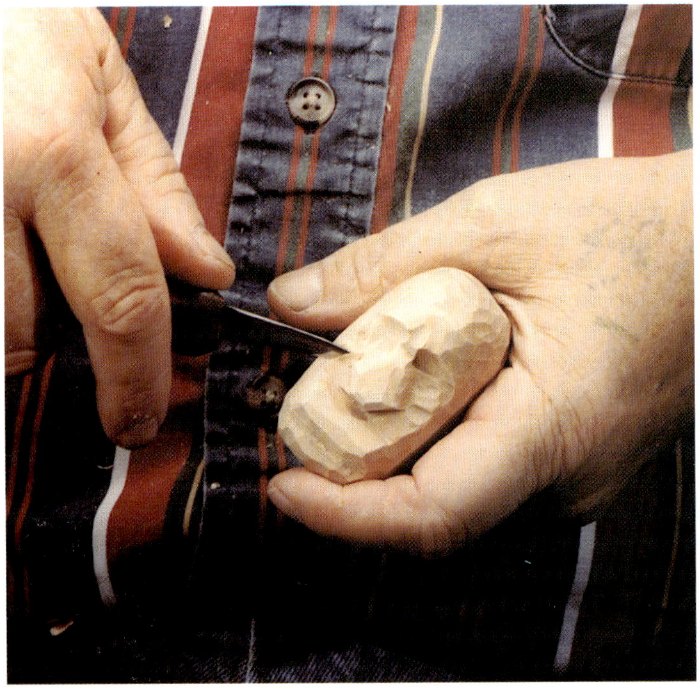

Come at it from the cheek line at a 45° angle.

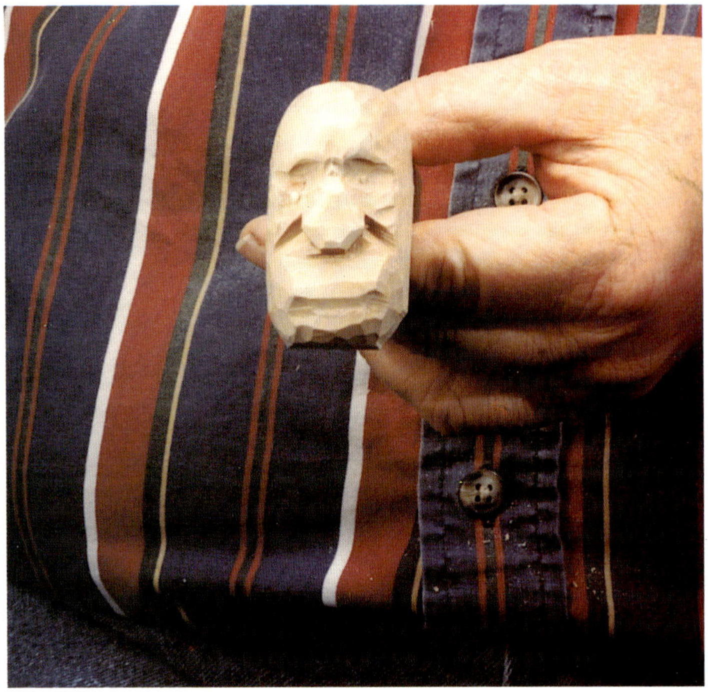

Progress.

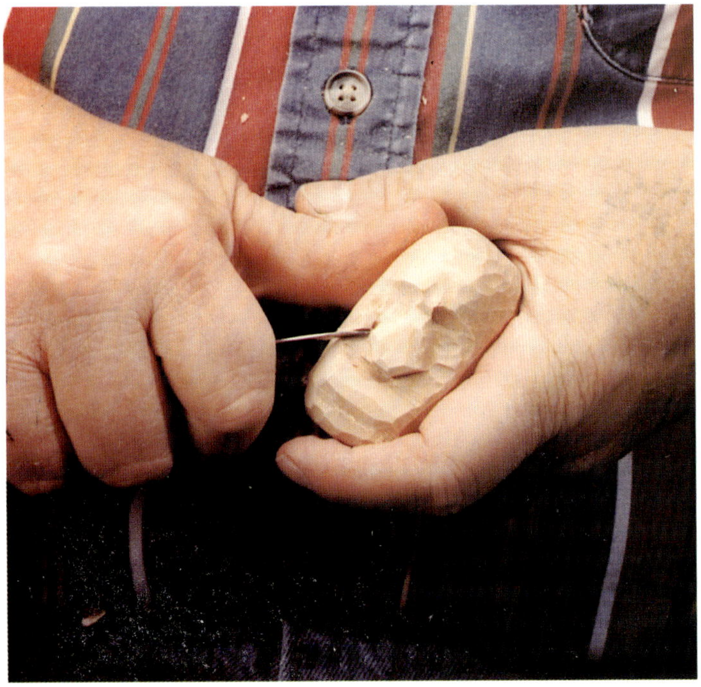

Then finish the triangle coming up from the mouth. The little piece should pop right out.

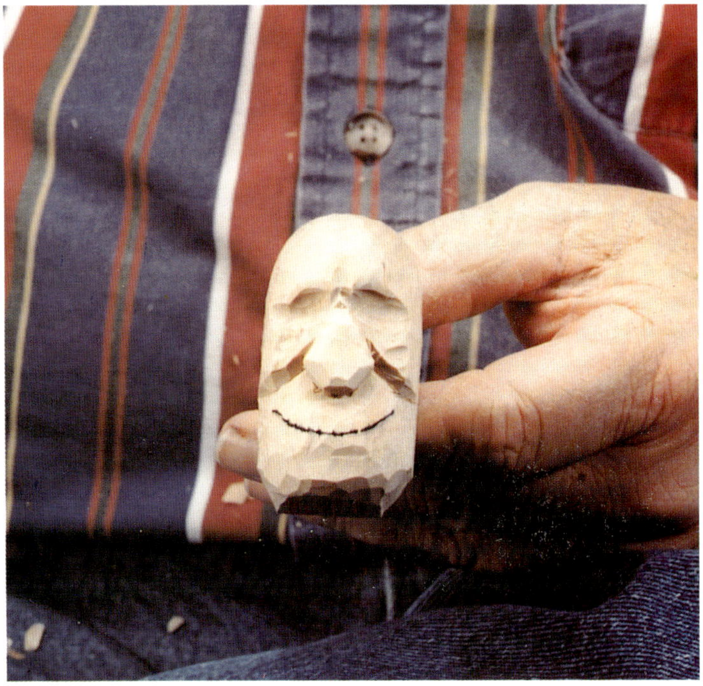

I'm marking a big smile for this one. When a person smiles, the lips don't turn up so much as they get wider. But for some reason, in caricature carving, we need to exaggerate the upturned corners.

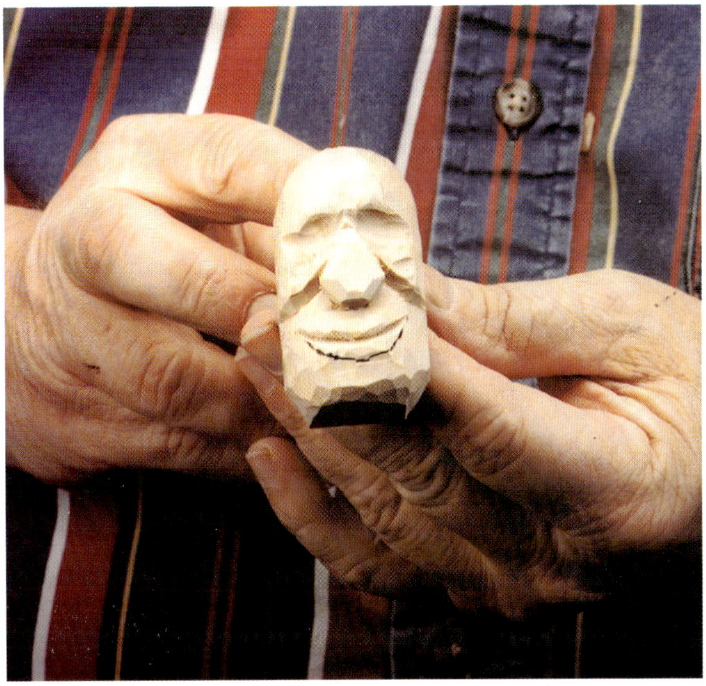

Make a cut line where you marked it. I have also marked the *upper edge* of the lower lip—I want a big toothy smile.

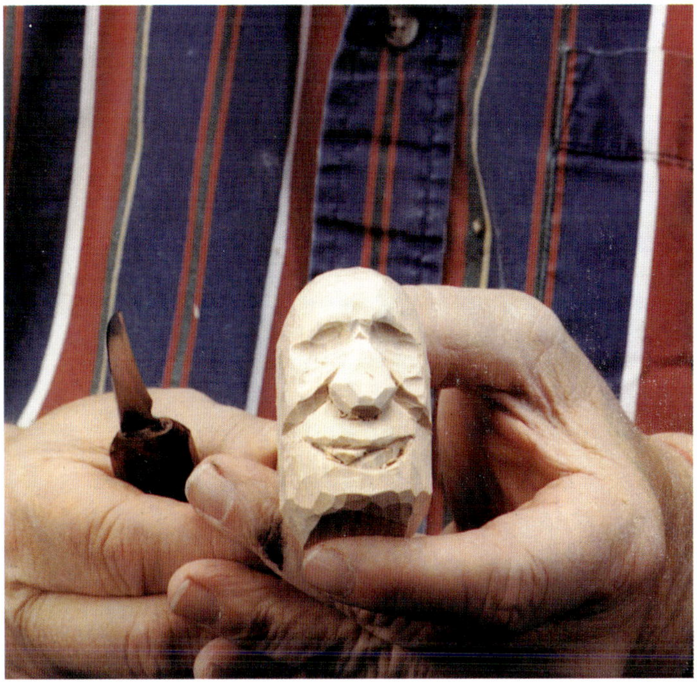

One cut all the way across makes the tongue come out of the corner of the mouth with some teeth in the other corner.

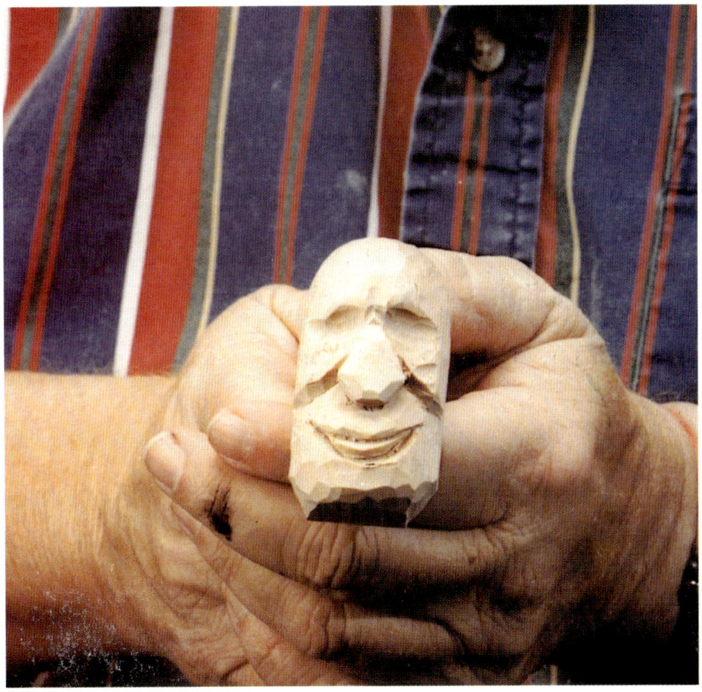

Make a cut along that line as well. You could stop the mouth here with a big tongue, or keep going—the possibilities are endless.

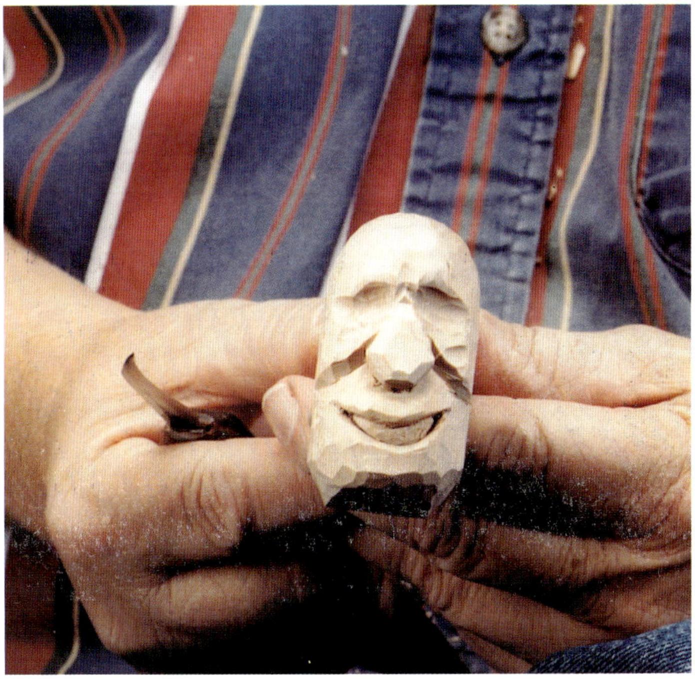

I'm going to take the tongue out altogether and give him some teeth. I'm cleaning up the edges of the lips before I do the individual teeth.

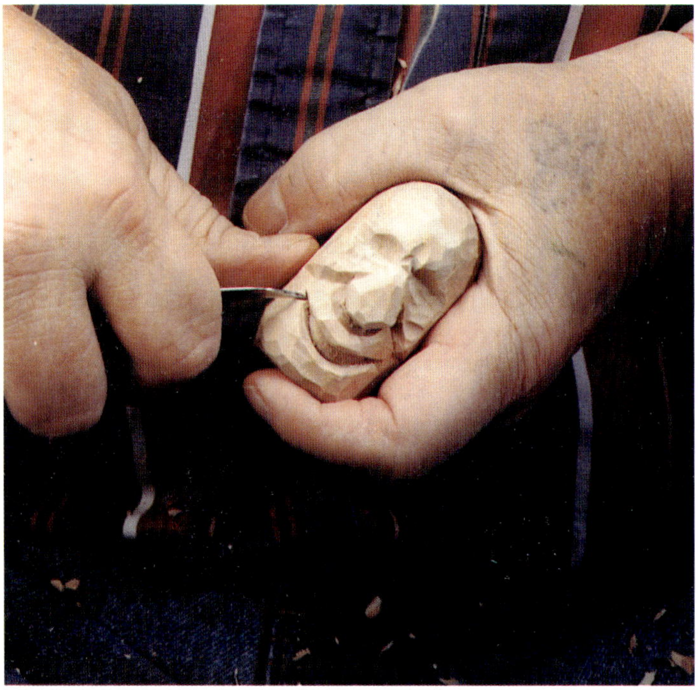

I'm notching out the corners of the mouth to make the lower lip go under the upper one.

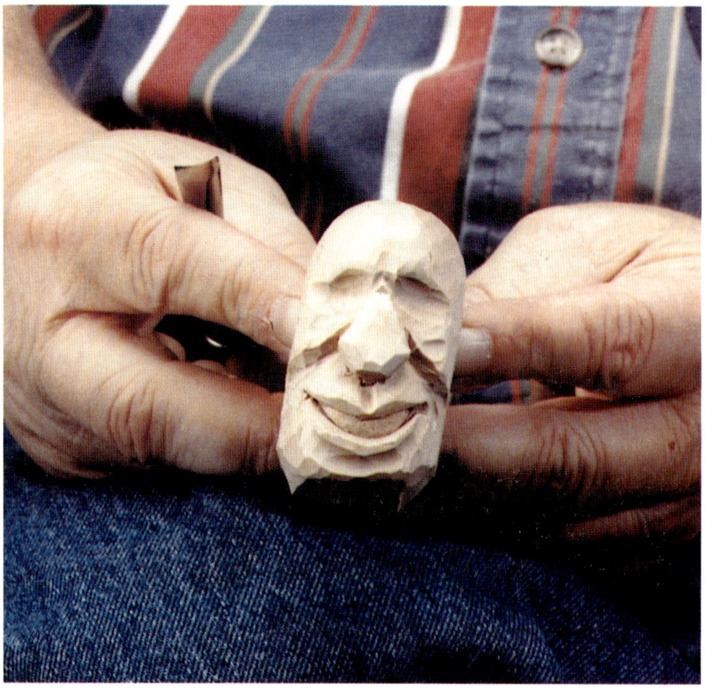

Outline the lips by cutting a shallow trench right above or below each lip—this makes them curl out.

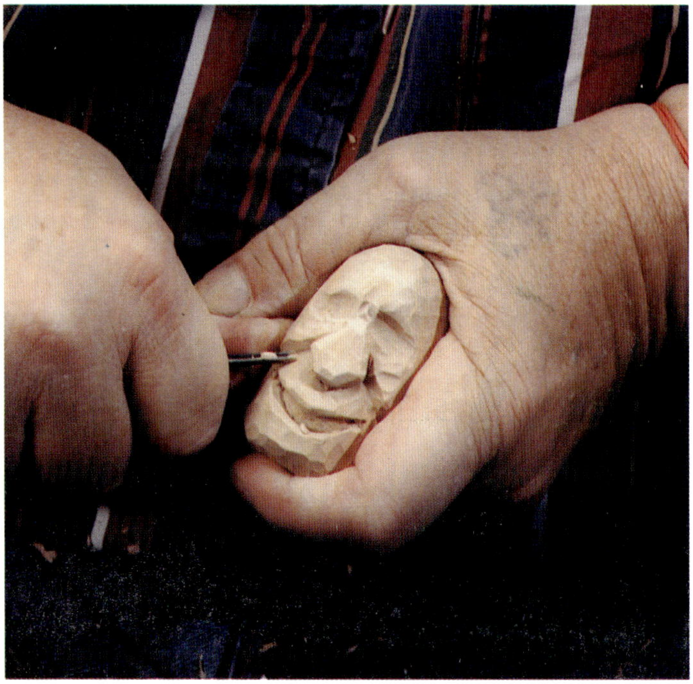

Make some smile lines around the corners of the mouth.

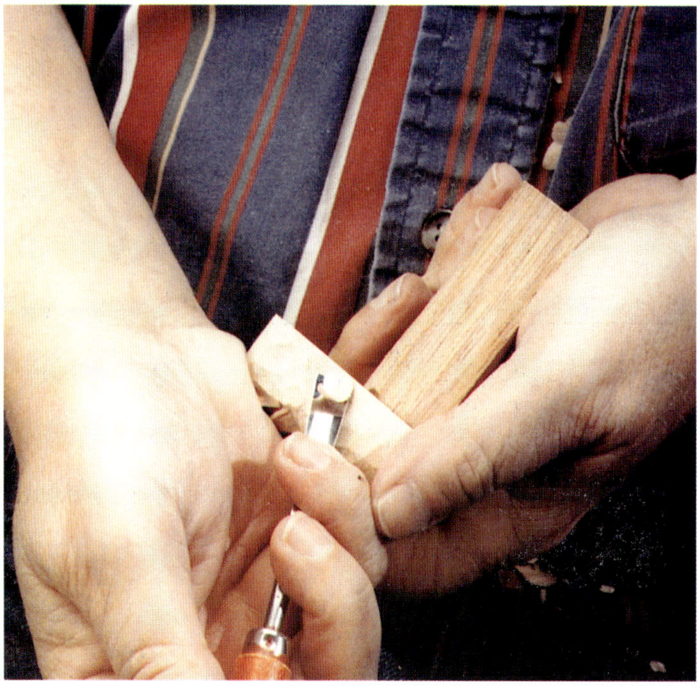

In order to dramatize the expression, he should have rounder smiley cheeks. Undercut all the way behind the cheeks to the edge.The cheeks should be the widest part of the face.

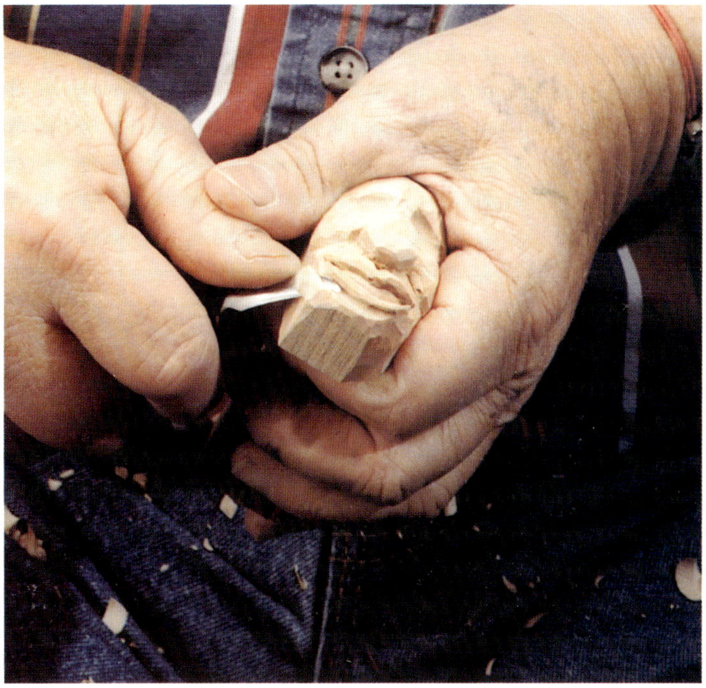

Narrowing the chin helps, too.

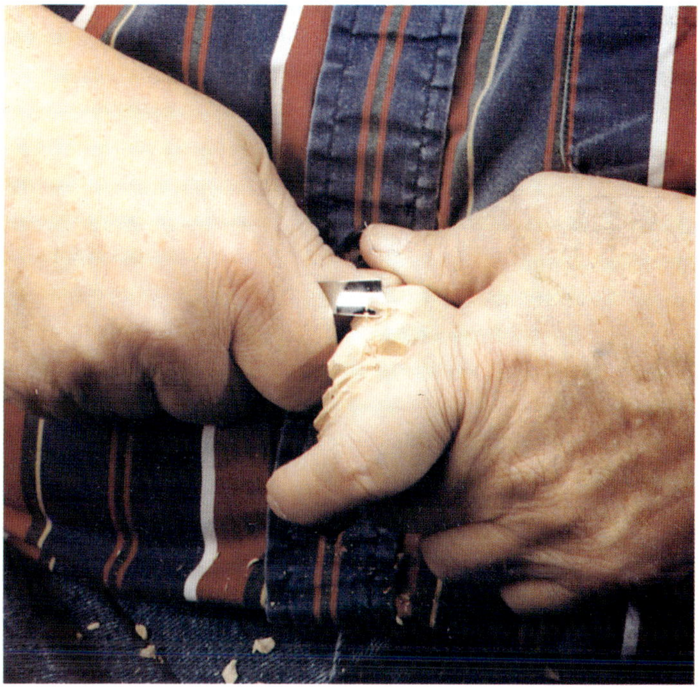

I'm also raising the eyebrows.

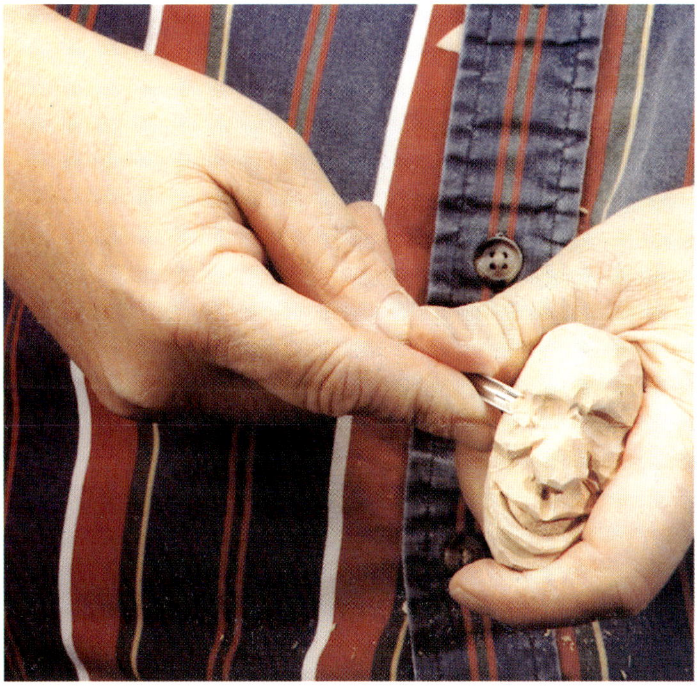

Round the cheeks out from the outer corner of the eye to the temple area.

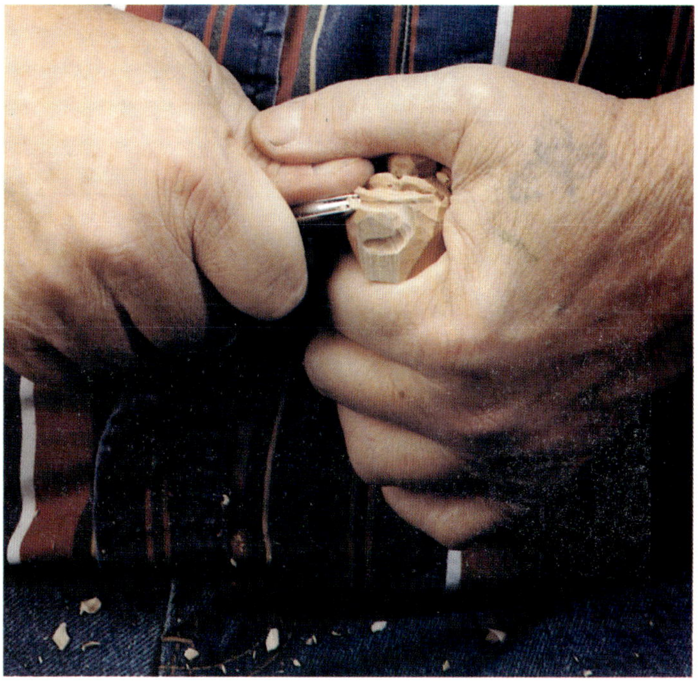

We should bring the chin out a little bit. Use a half round gouge to outline the chin.

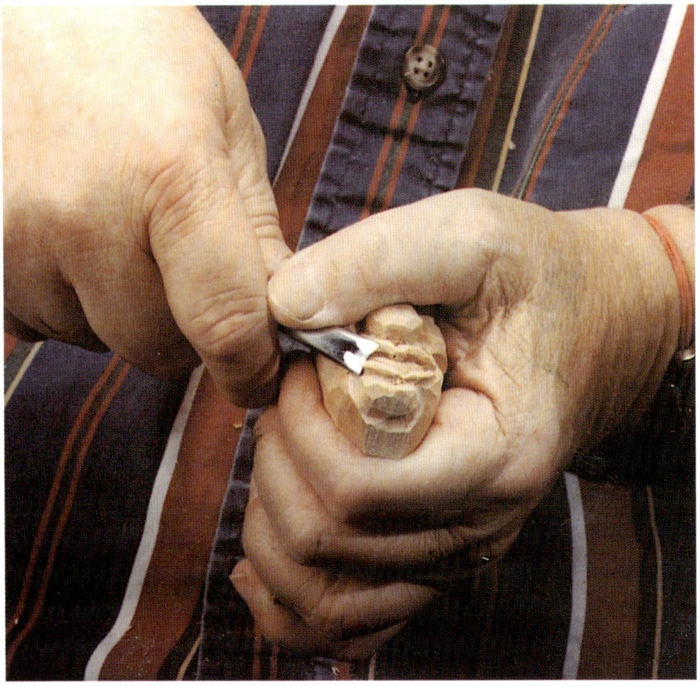

The lips are a little sharp looking, so I'll round them.

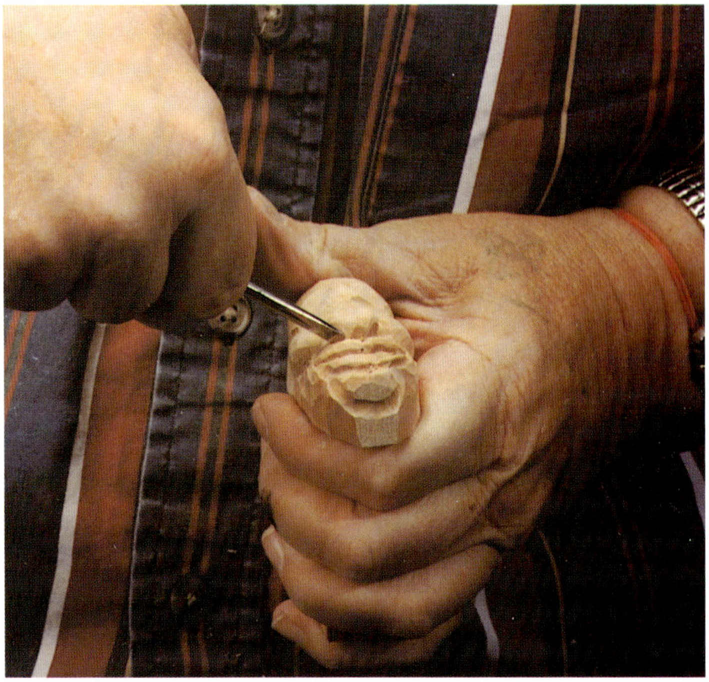

I'm going to make a wider but shallower cut for the nostrils. I'm using a flatter gouge to make them flare out in a laughing way.

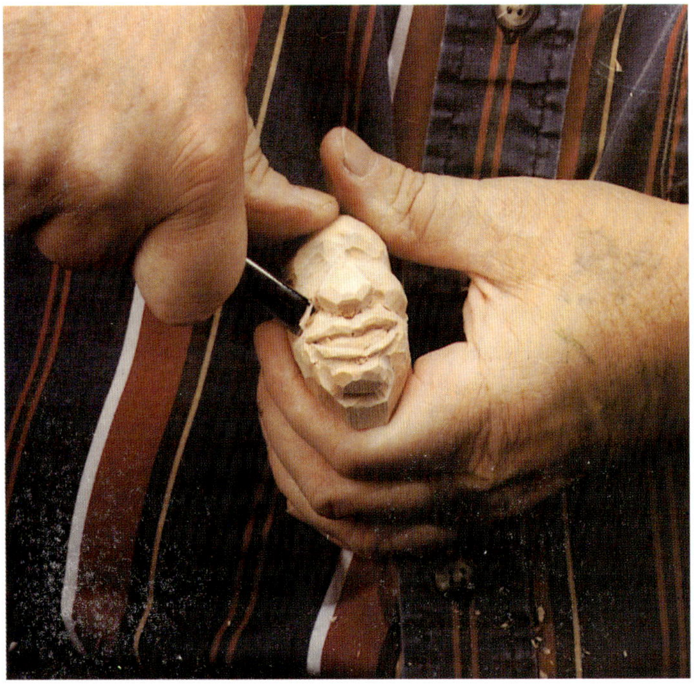

The cheeks are hard-looking, so we'll round them out some too.

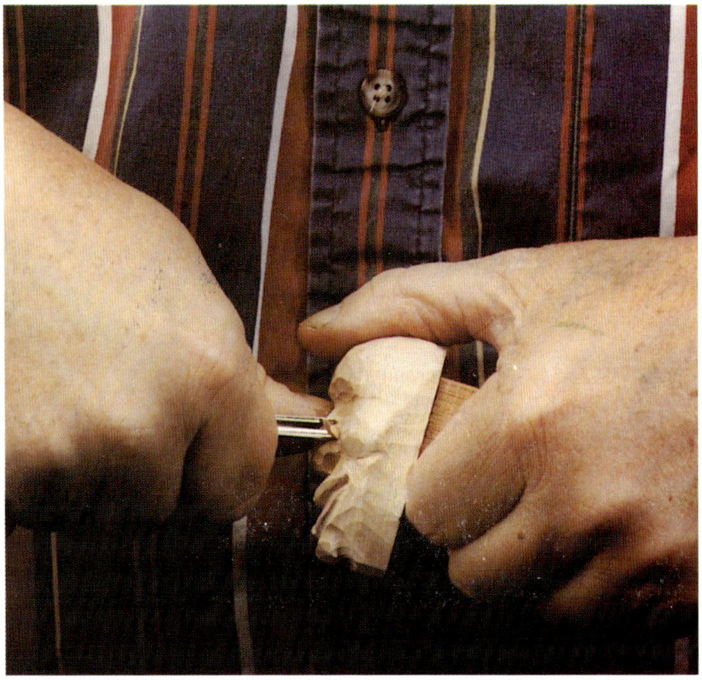

I'm using a half round to bring out those nostrils a little better.

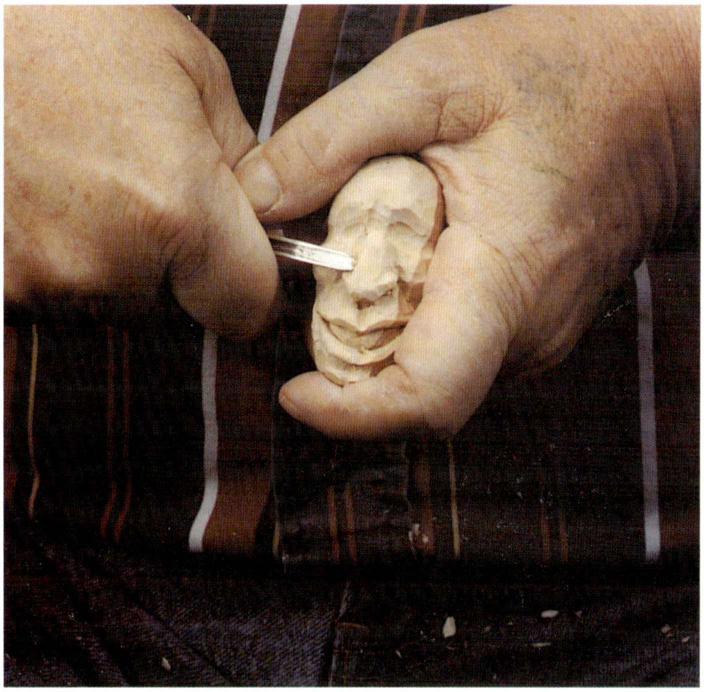

The veiner can make a mark to finish the nostrils in a nice line.

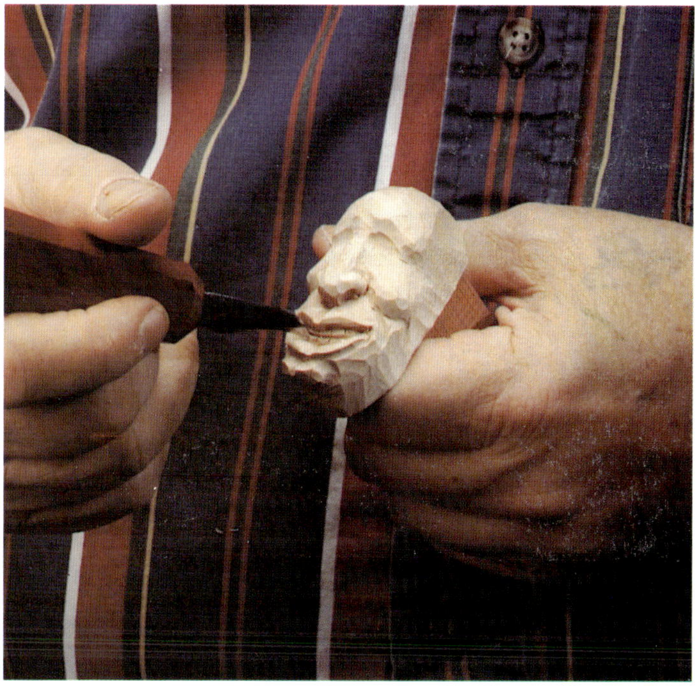

A hooked knife is perfect to make the marks between the teeth.

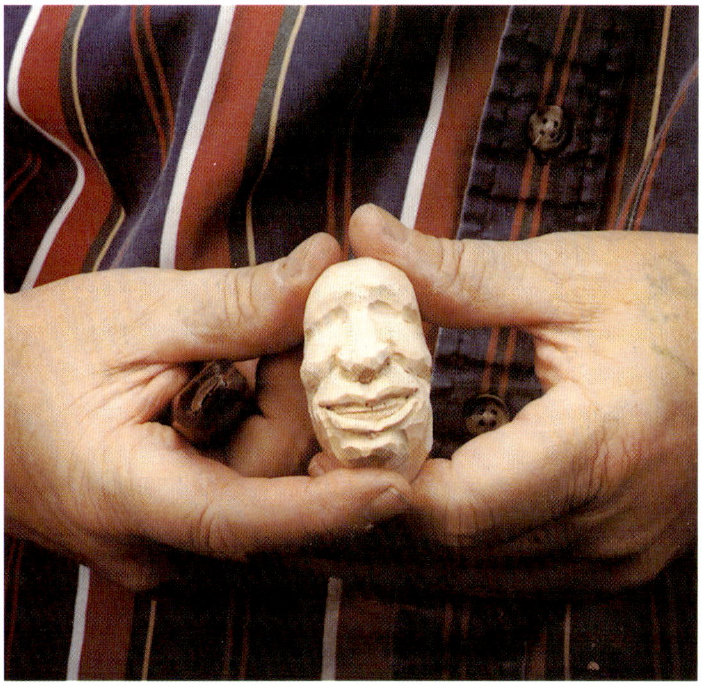

Progress. To make the line where the teeth bite together, you can make two cuts with a knife. I have a 24° V-Tool (by Charles Berold) that gets the job done twice as fast.

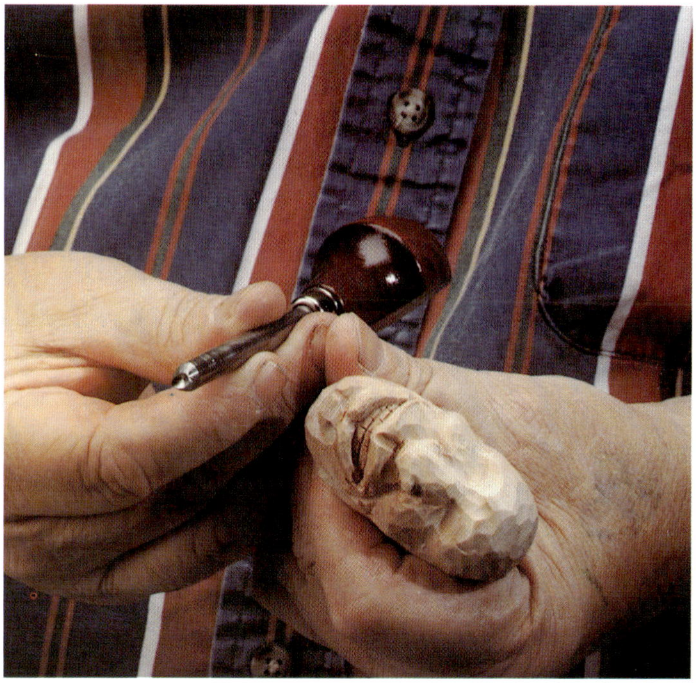

I ground this eye punch for more of an almond shape.

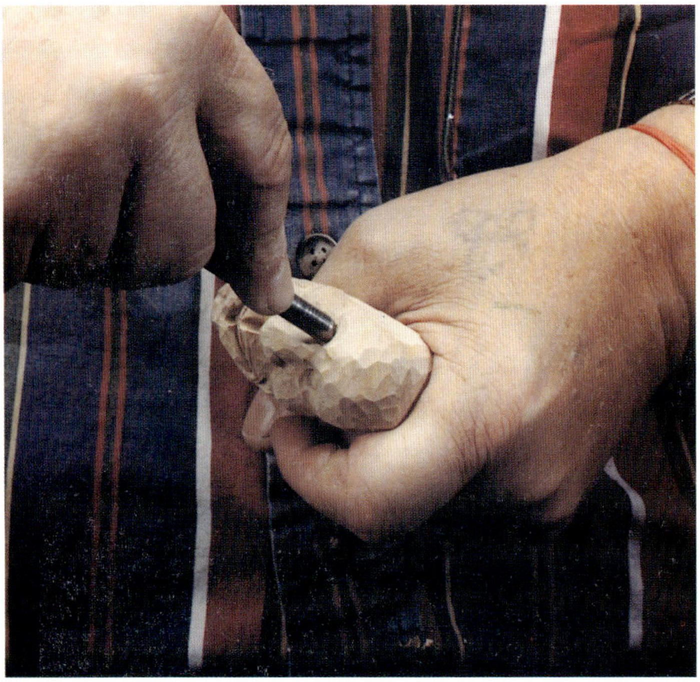

Punching the eye.

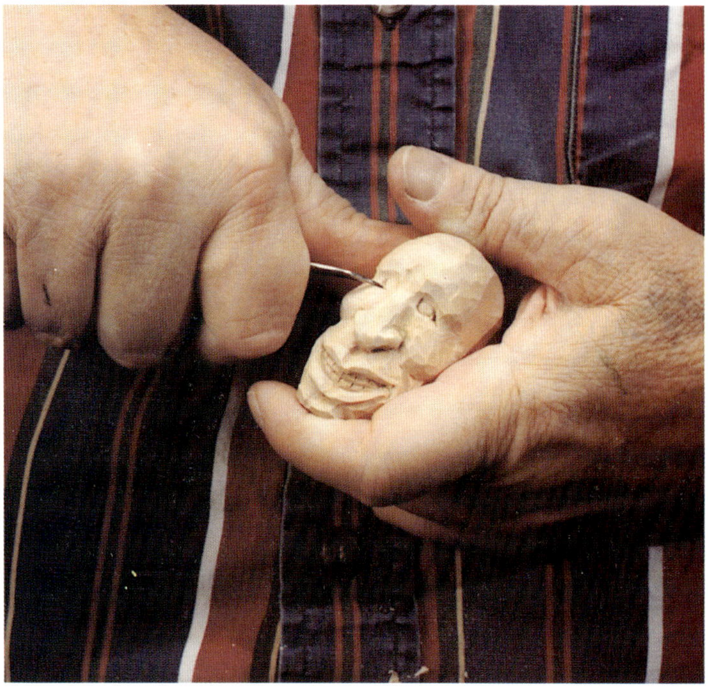

For the laugh lines at the corners of the eyes, I'm using the same three-cut method I used on the nose and corner of the mouth. Start with a cut straight down, cut from each end of it at 45°, and pop the little triangle out.

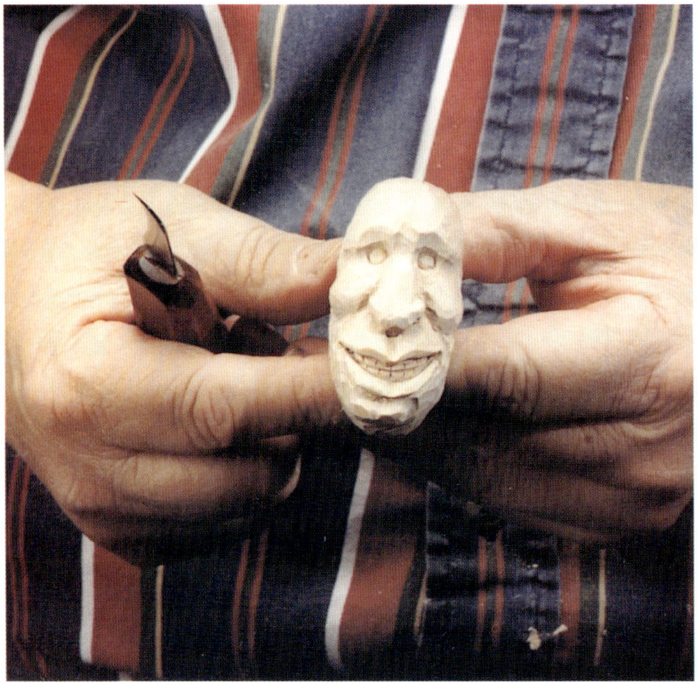

Progress.

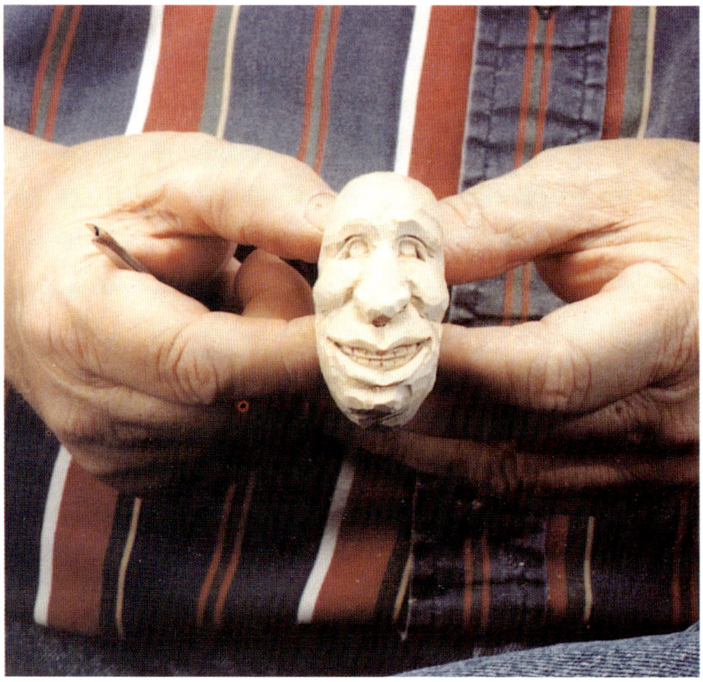

Progress. I went around the top of the eye with the veiner to make eyelids.

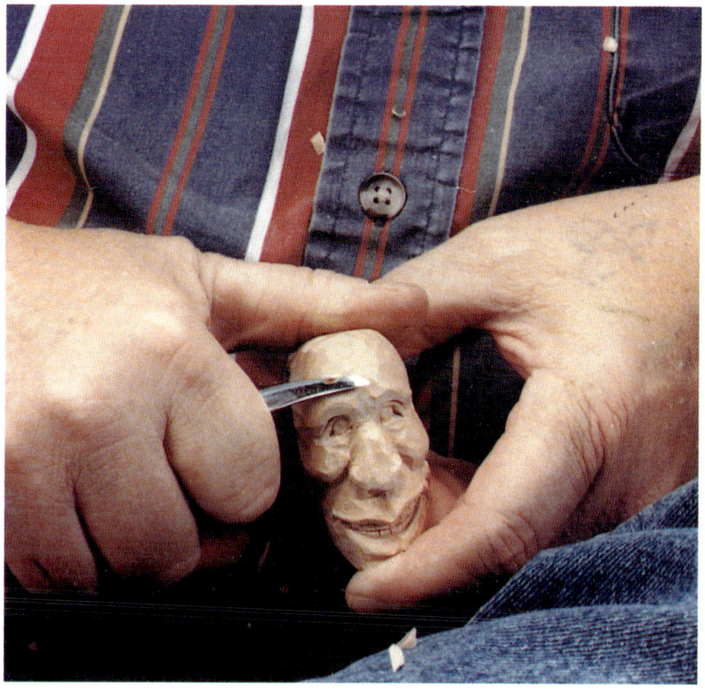

I want to change the eyebrows. I'm reshaping the forehead.

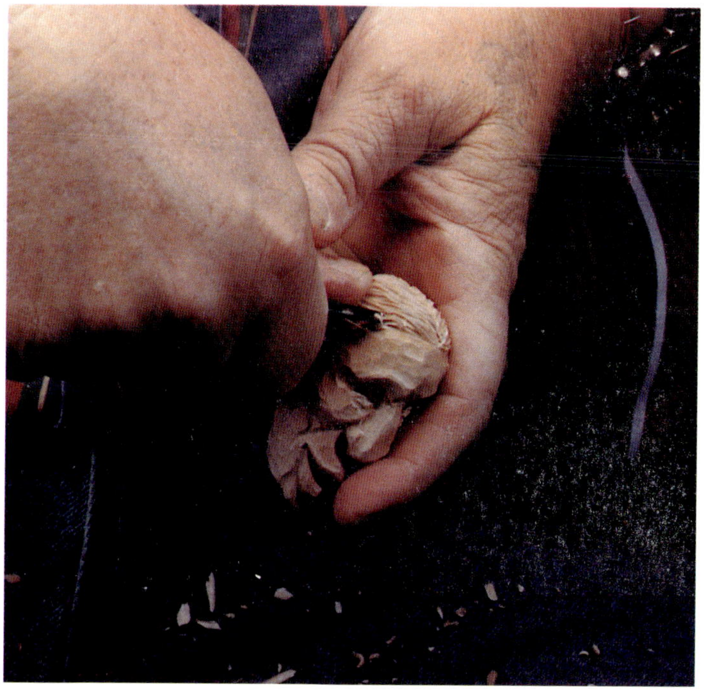

The veiner gives the hair and eyebrows some texture.

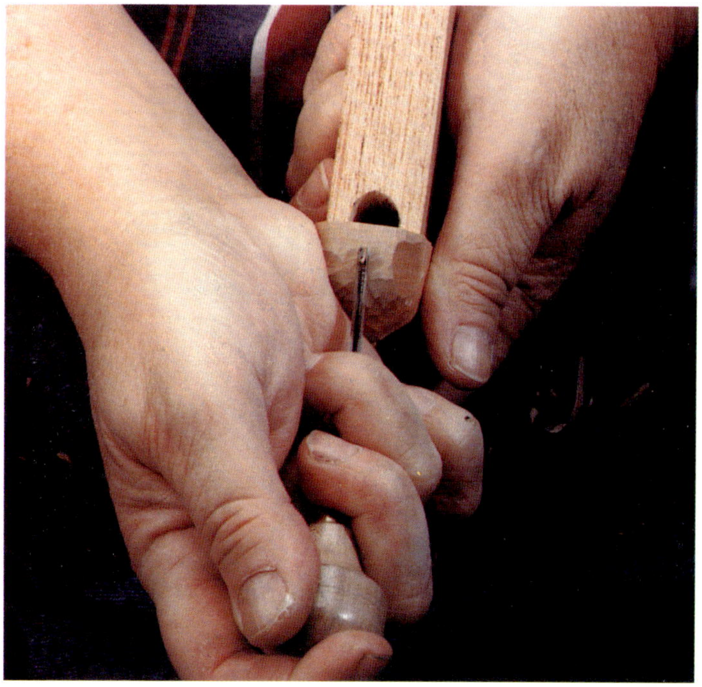

I'm using the V-tool to make a hairline and a part.

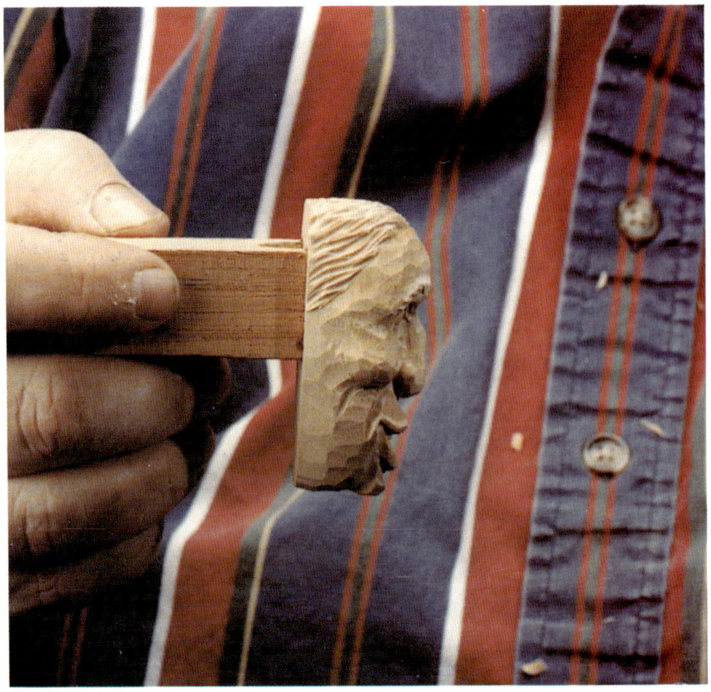

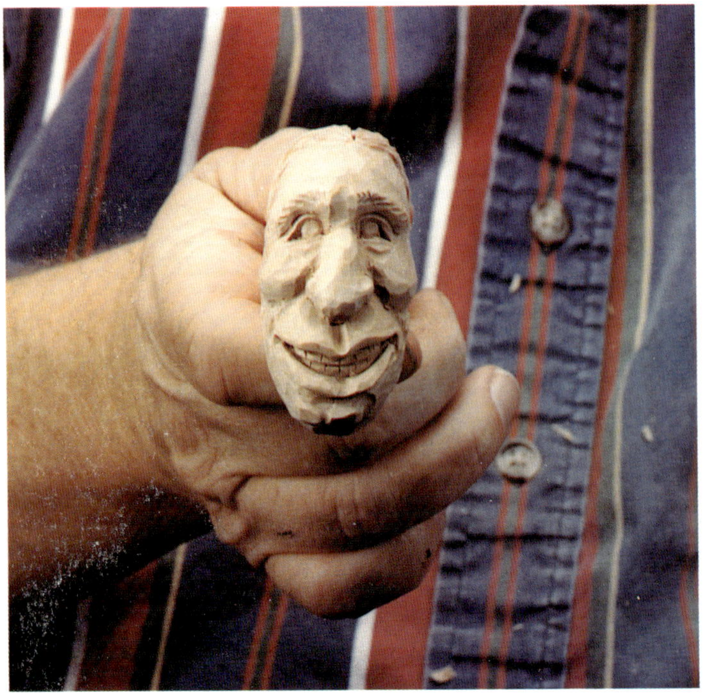

The finished carving.

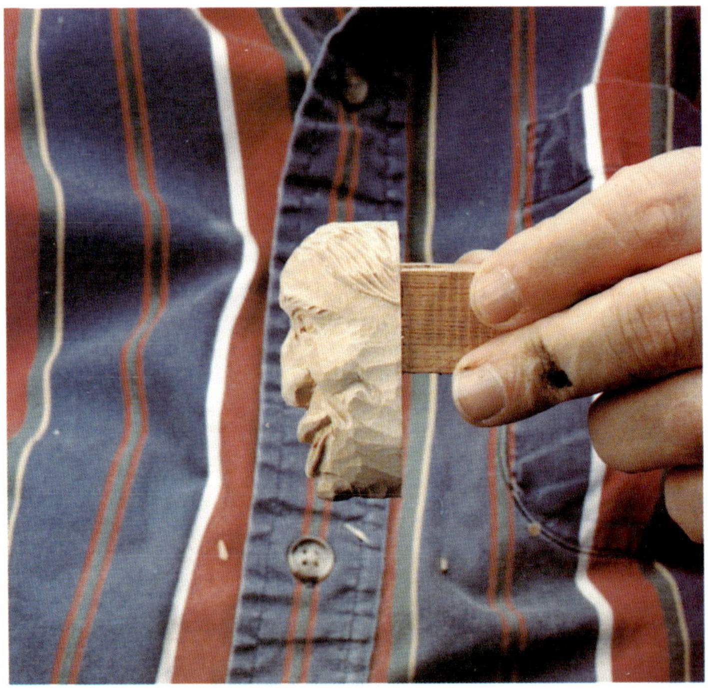

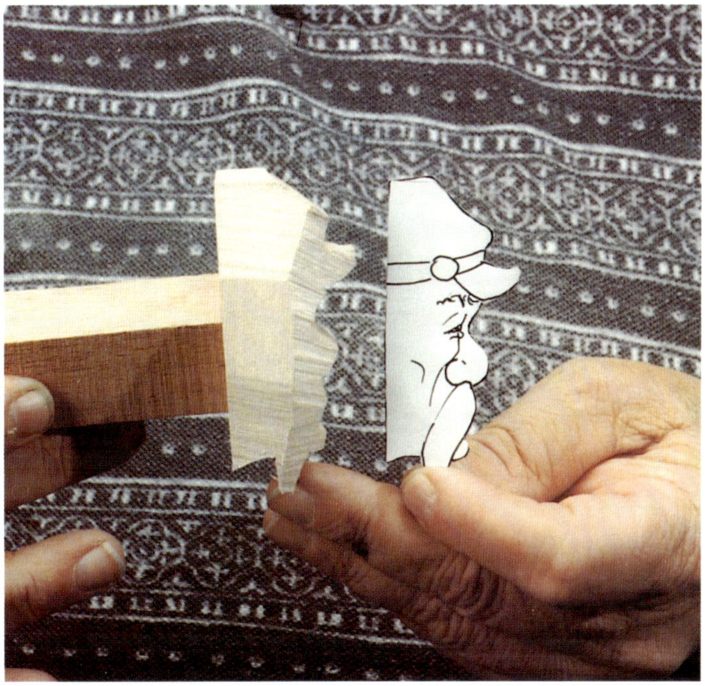

Our next project will be from a pattern. It's a tribute to the spirit of the confederacy!

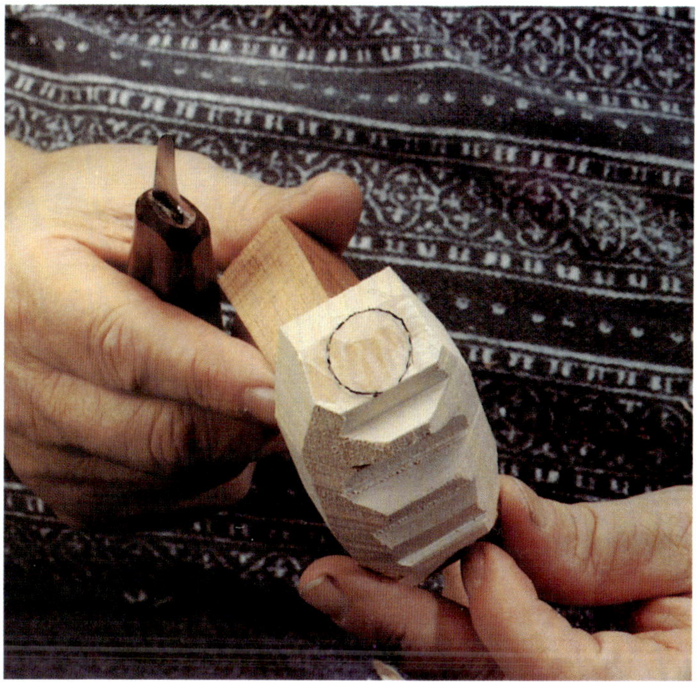

I'm beginning by marking the kepi.

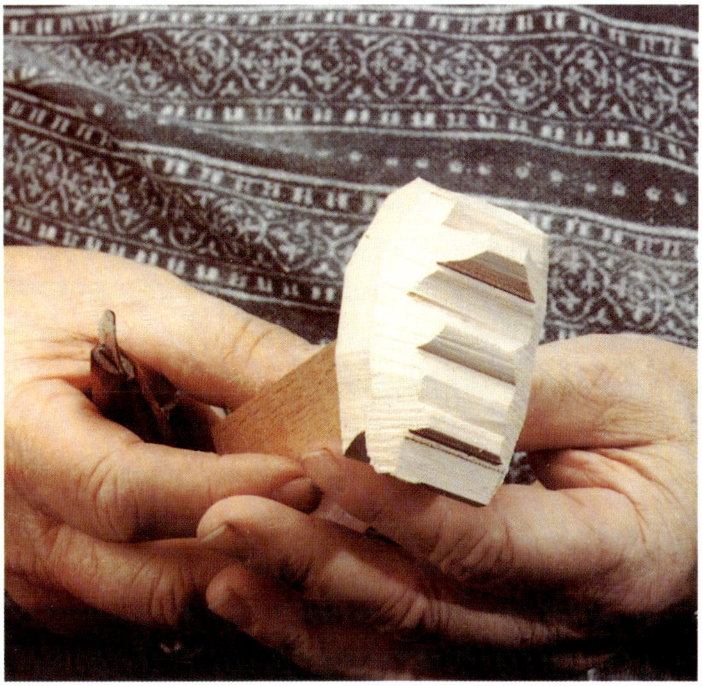

I used the bandsaw at a 45° angle to knock off the edges here.

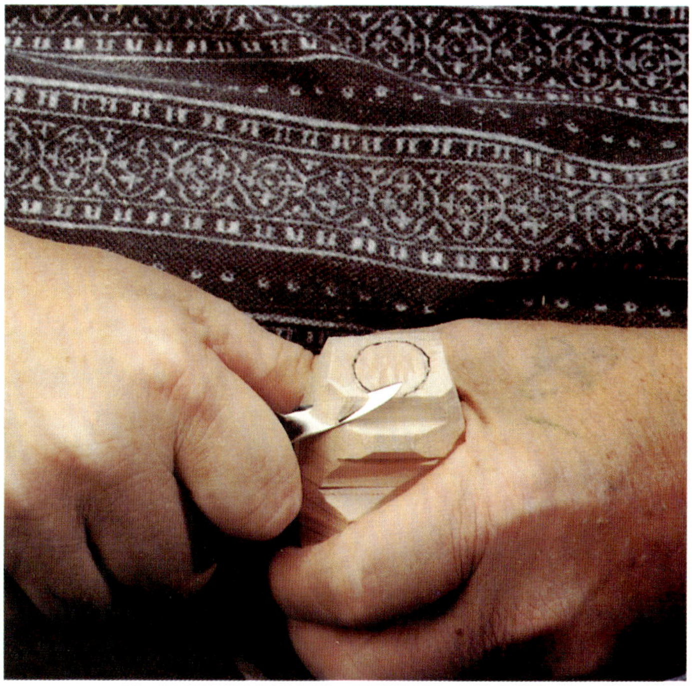

Now I'm cutting back to it.

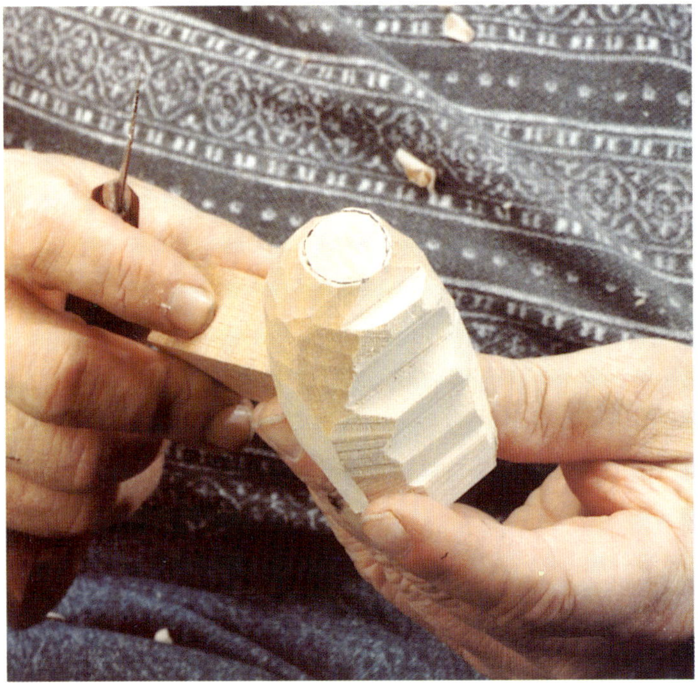

Progress.

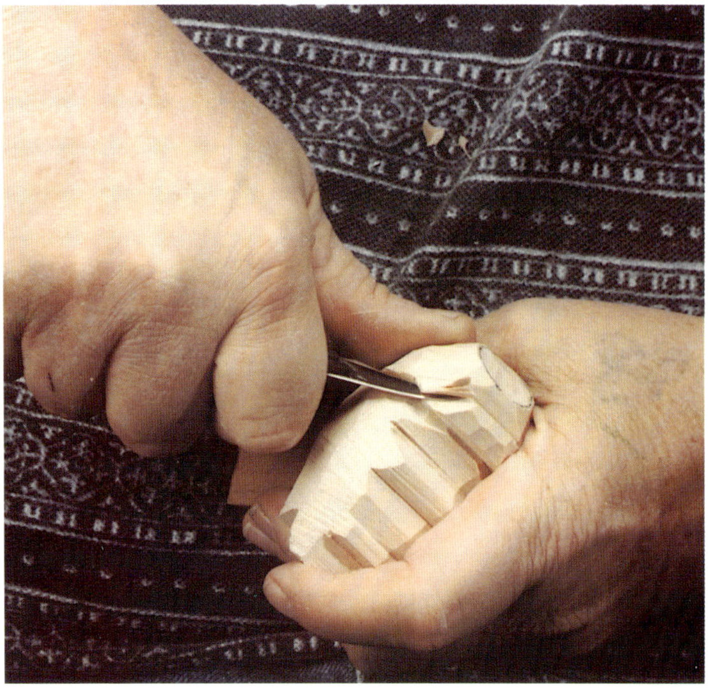

I'm cutting into the bill to thin it out.

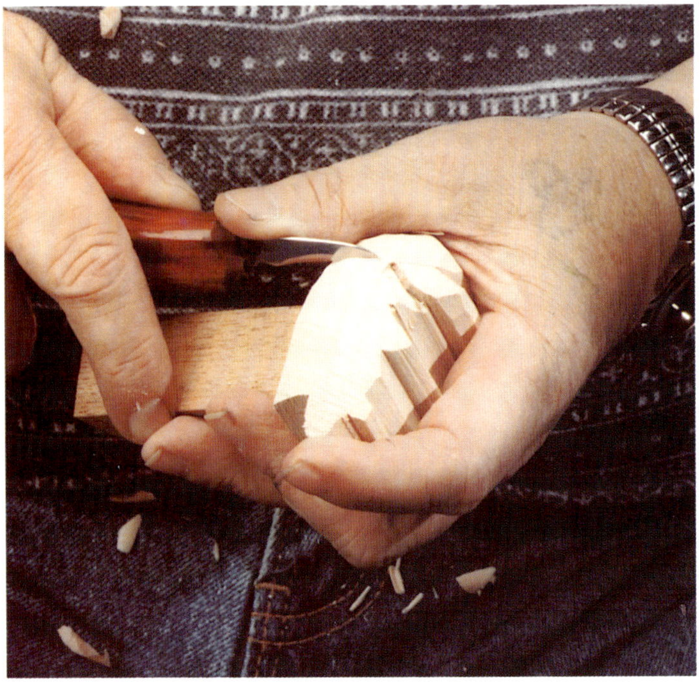

Make a stop cut all the way around the cap.

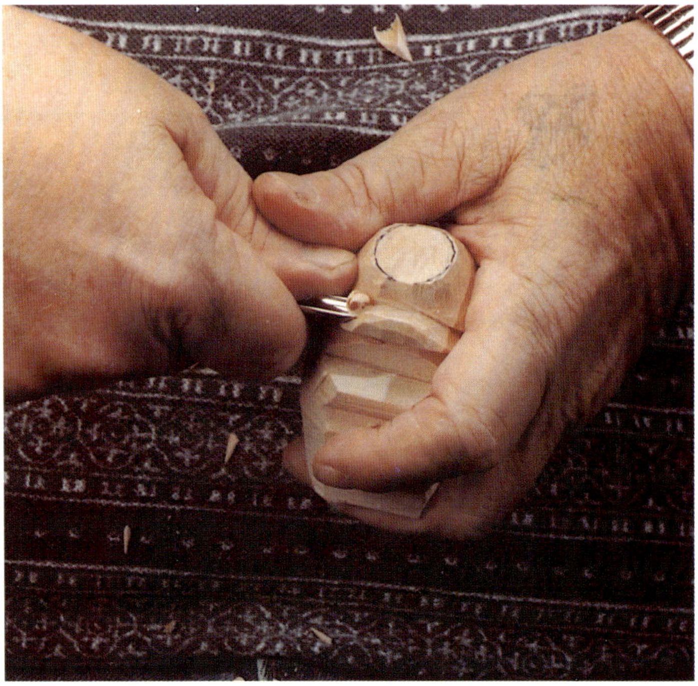

I'm using a gouge to cut around the upper side of the bill to really give it some curl.

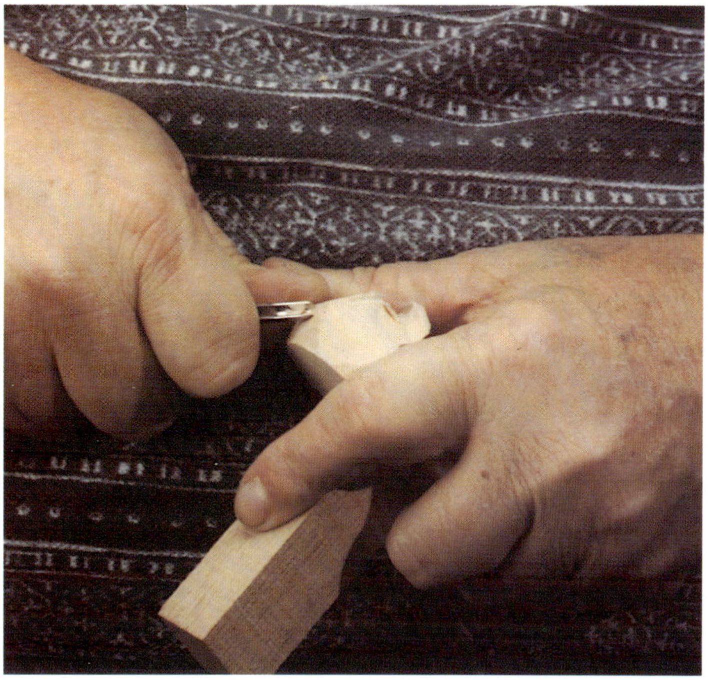

The cap has a flat part sewn on top of it. I'm using a veiner to make the seam.

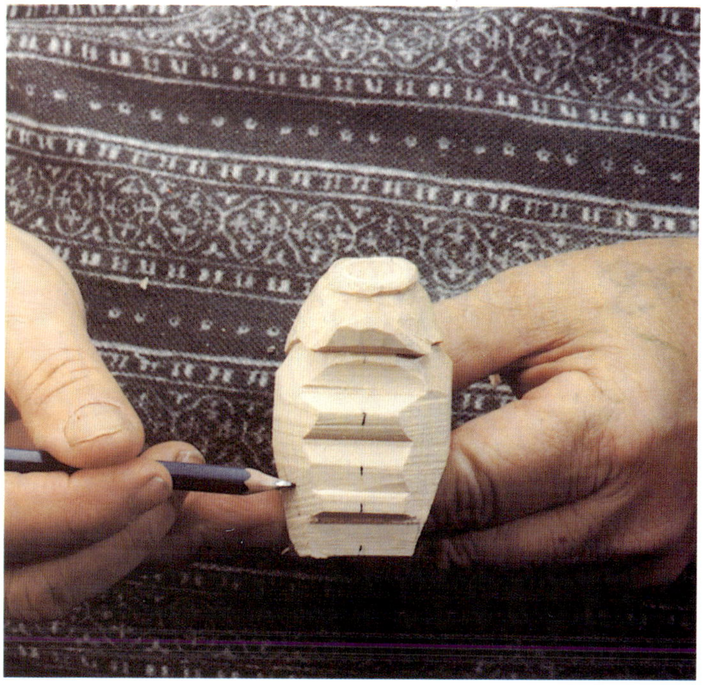

Mark a center line for the face. This side looks heavy, so I'll cut it down some.

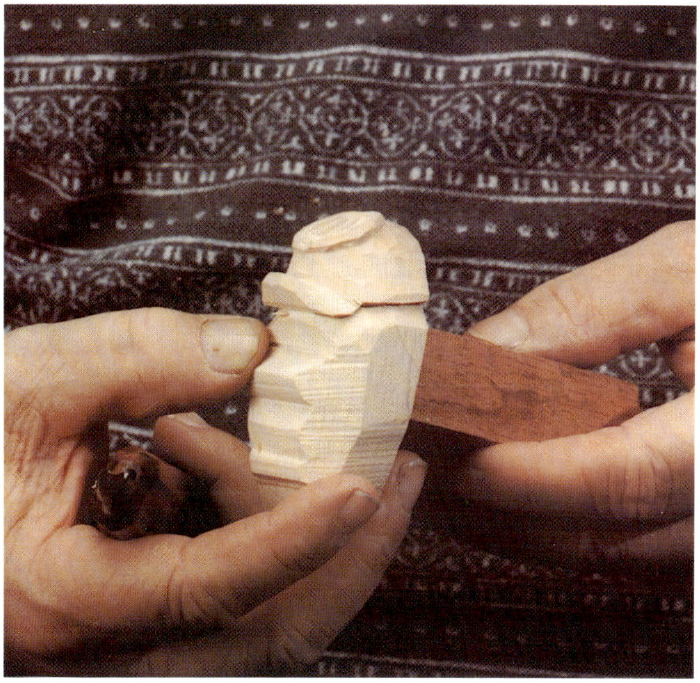

Progress.

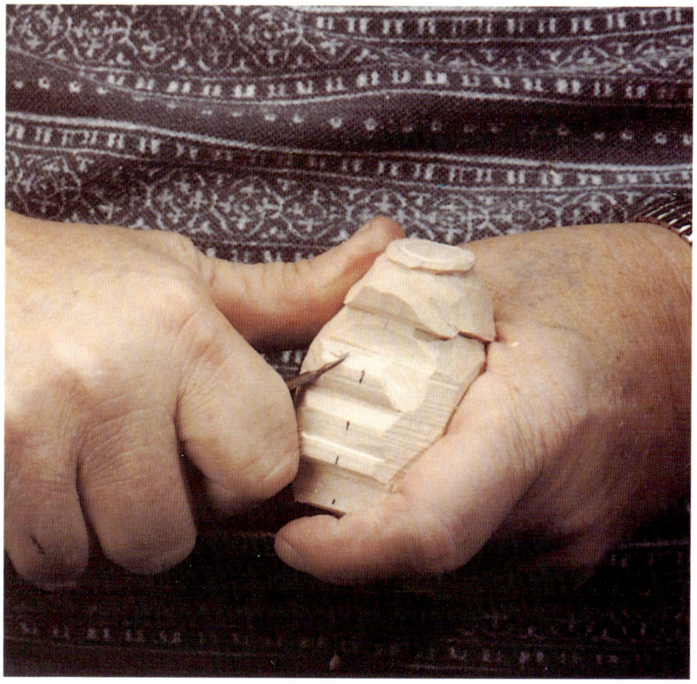

I'm coming up alongside the nose, leaving it good and heavy.

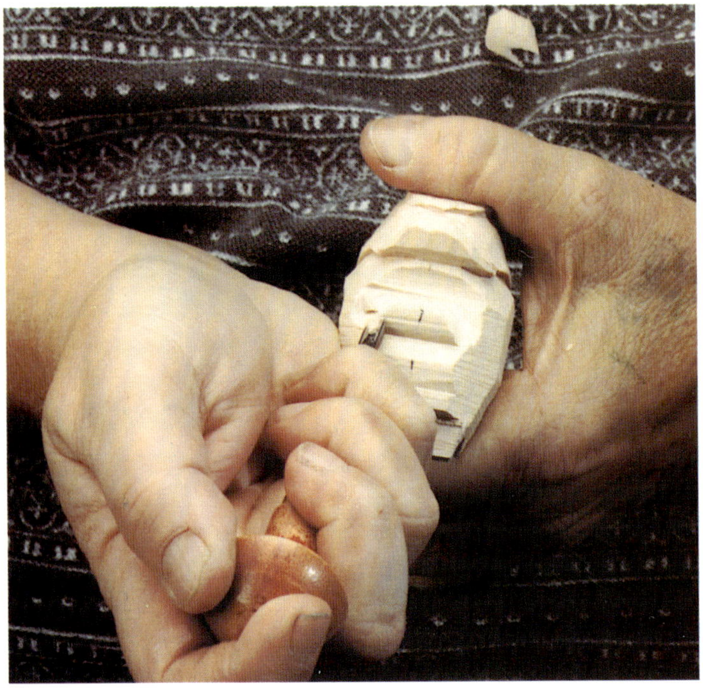

Size up the nose and make sure it's the same on both sides.

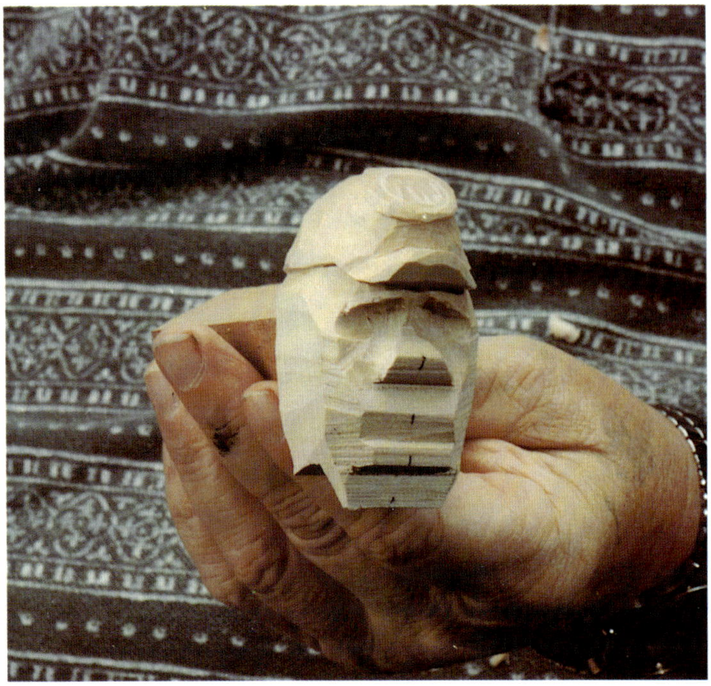

Progress.

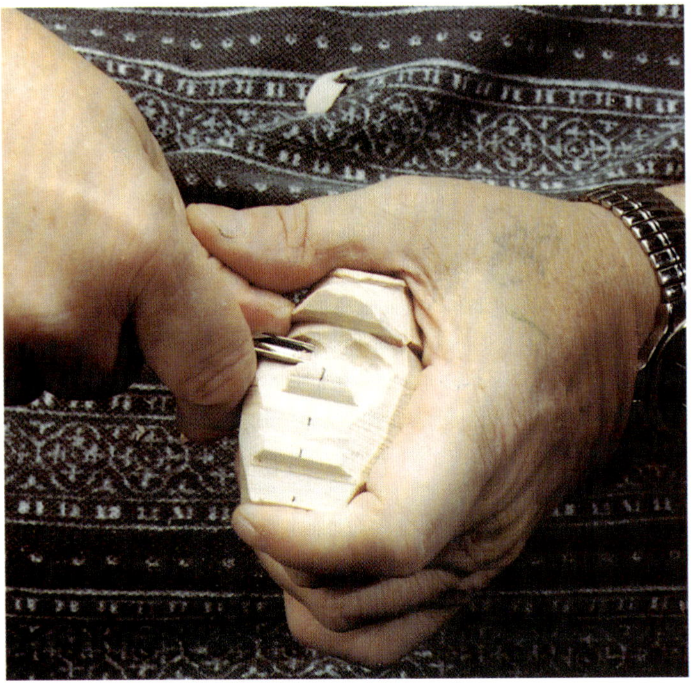

I'm digging into the eye sockets with a gouge to bring out the bridge of the nose.

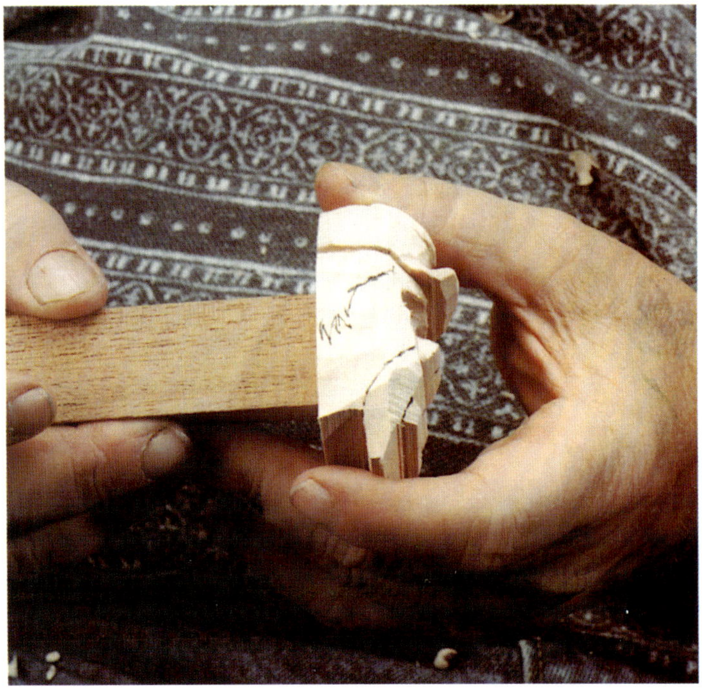

Now I'm marking the hair and moustache.

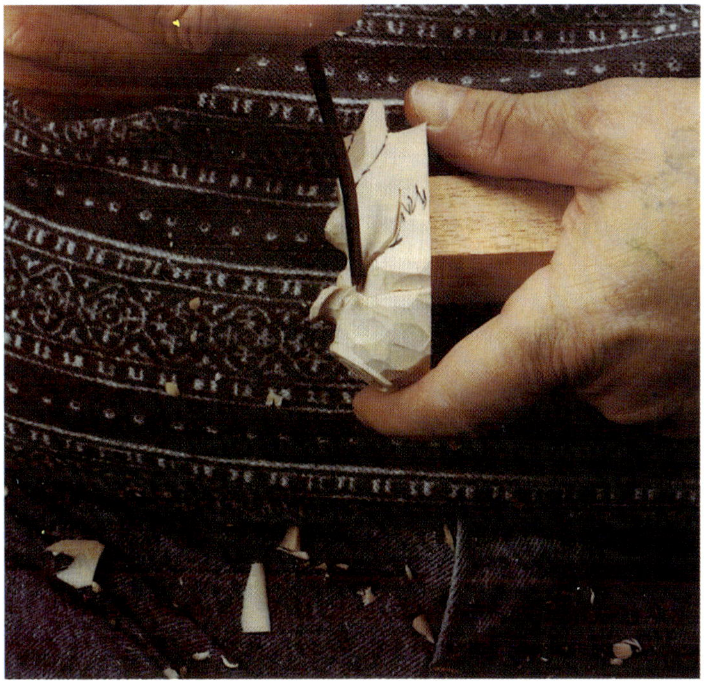

I'm using a V-tool to outline the hair, using the V-cut like a stop cut. I'm working back to it from the face. This also takes weight off the face, which should only be as wide as the bill of the cap.

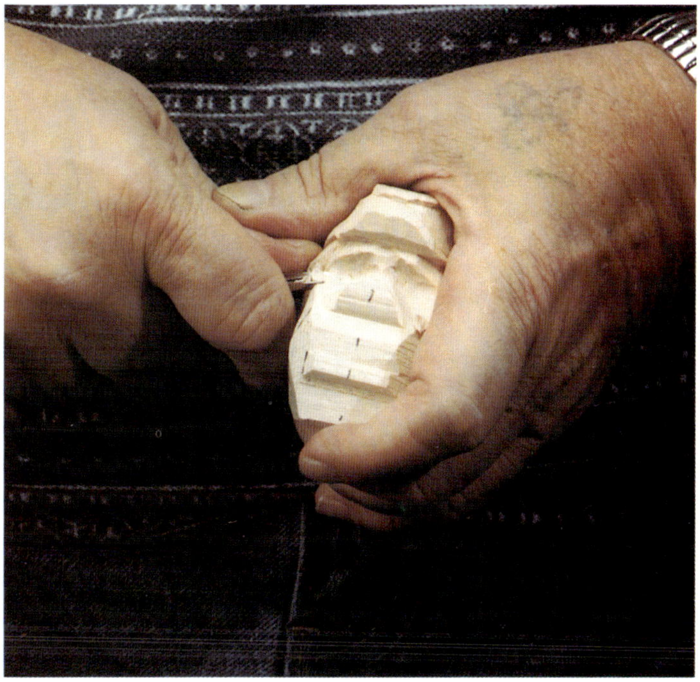

Cut from the temple in towards the eye socket to bring out the eyebrow (it might be easier to go the other direction). If you're looking for a more hollow look to the eye, don't cut these ridges.

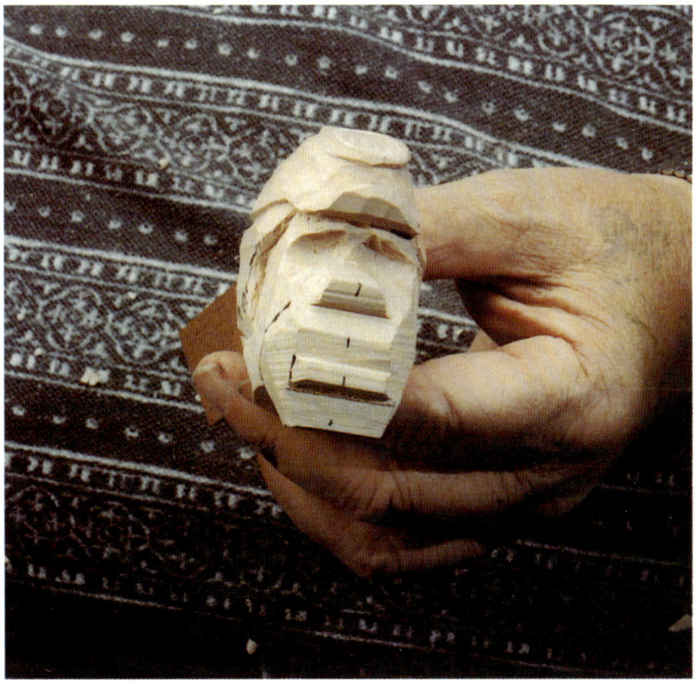

Progress.

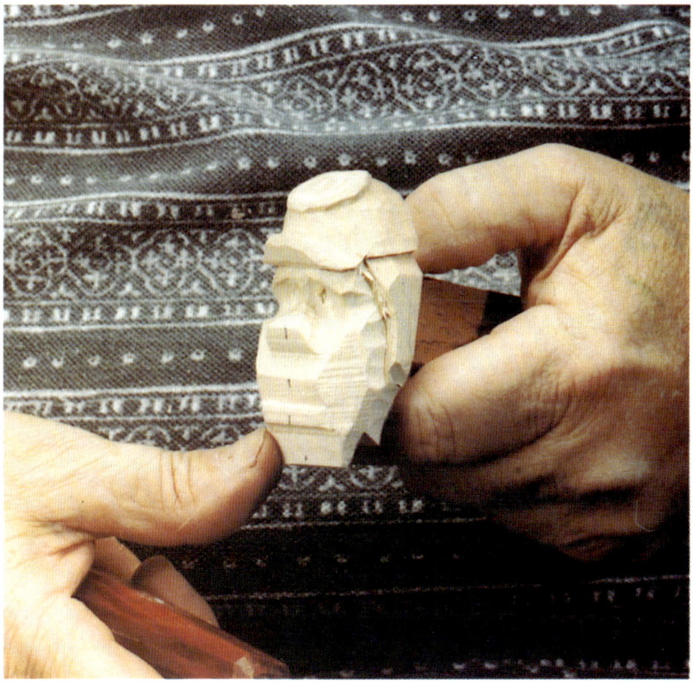

Progress.

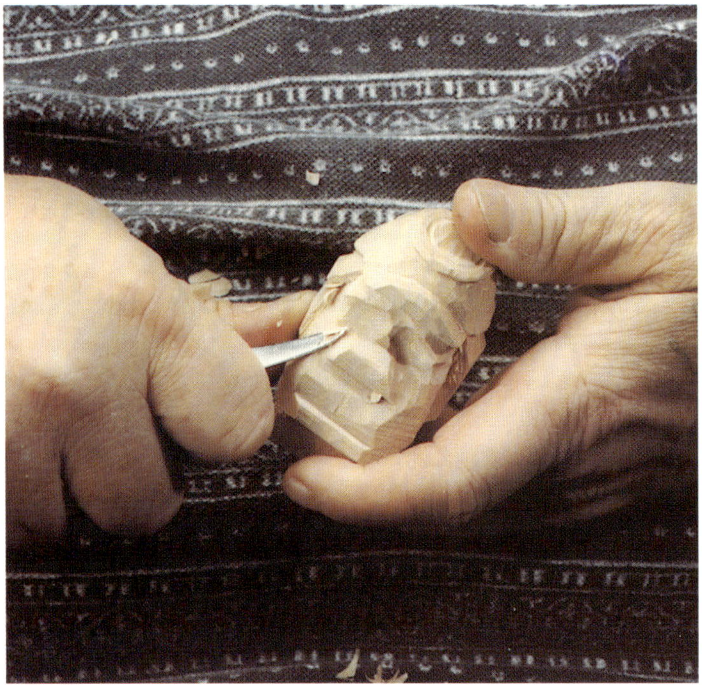

I'm cleaning up the face; rounding off sharp edges, saw marks, and pen marks.

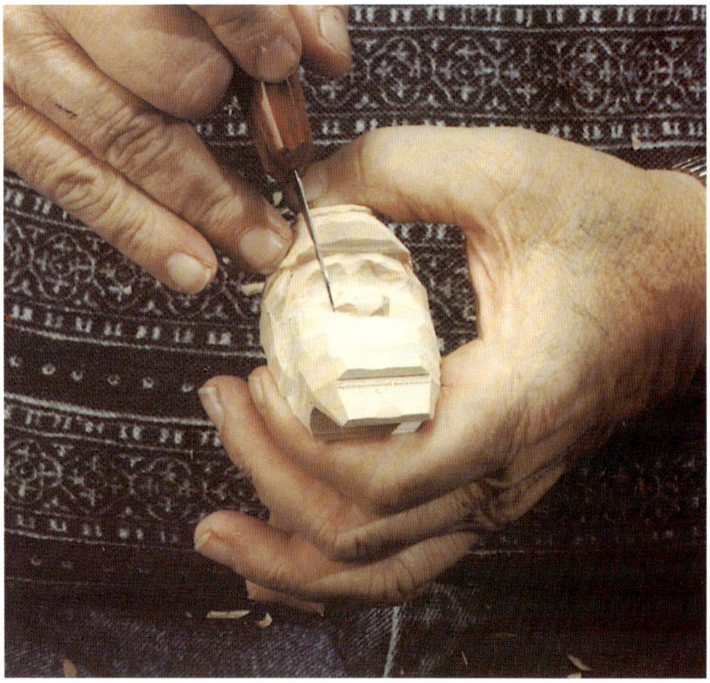

I'm making the triangle cut we've been using for the nose. Start with a cut straight down, and then come at it at 45° angles from the both the cheek and the moustache lines to make a triangle. I'm really bringing this one down to accomodate a big bushy moustache.

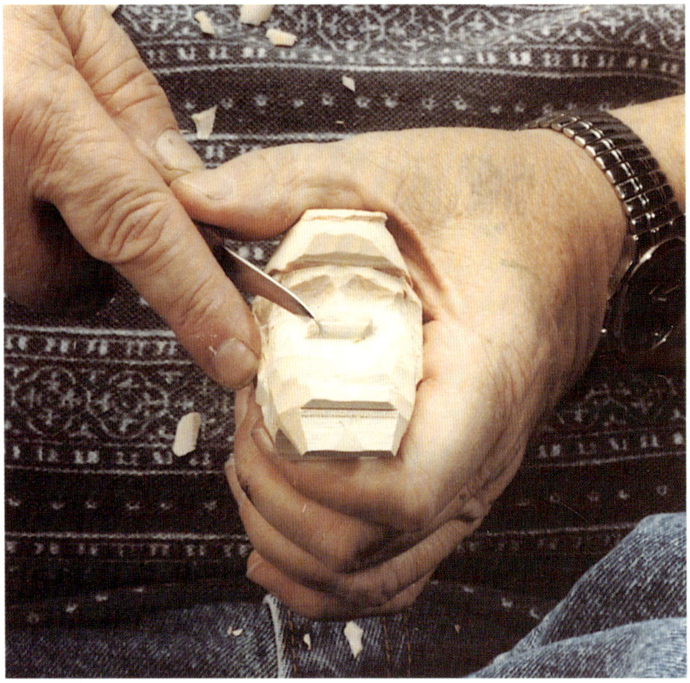

Knock off the corners of the nose to make nostrils.

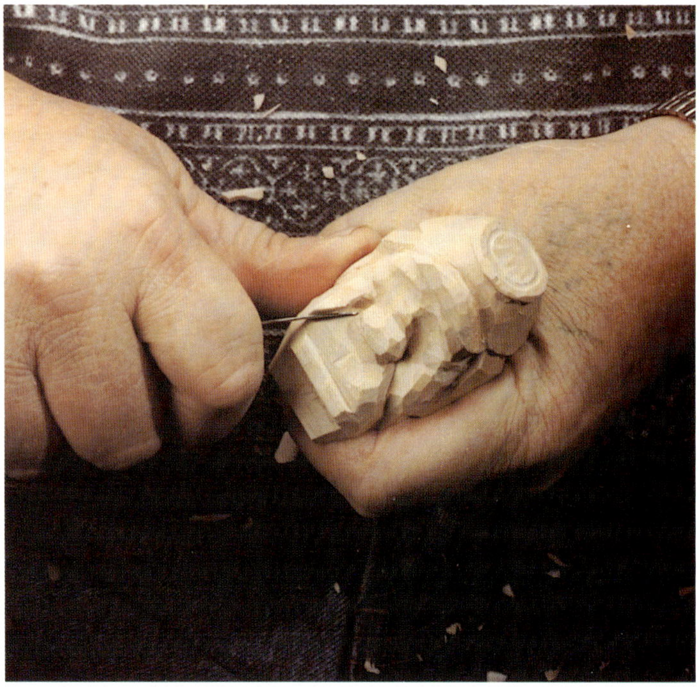

Bring this line all the way down along the moustache.

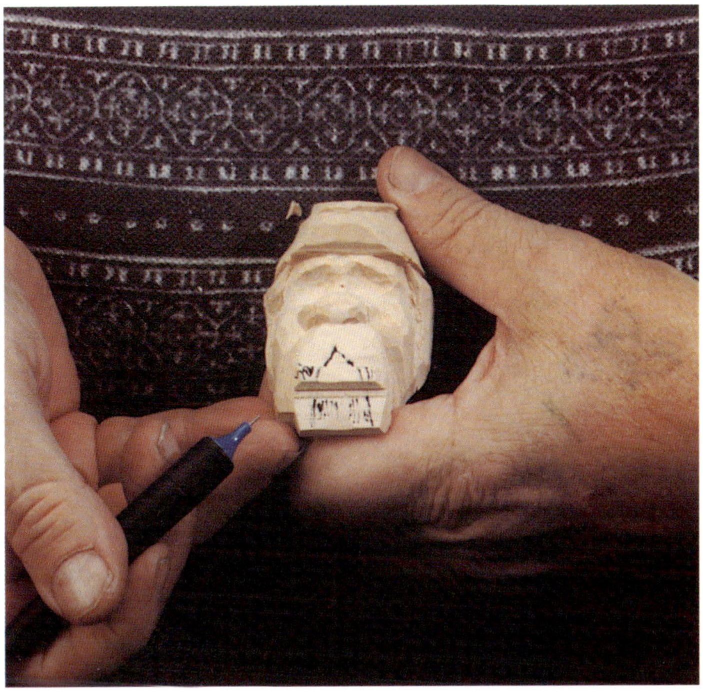

I'm marking the area to be cut inside the moustache. Be sure you leave room for the chin.

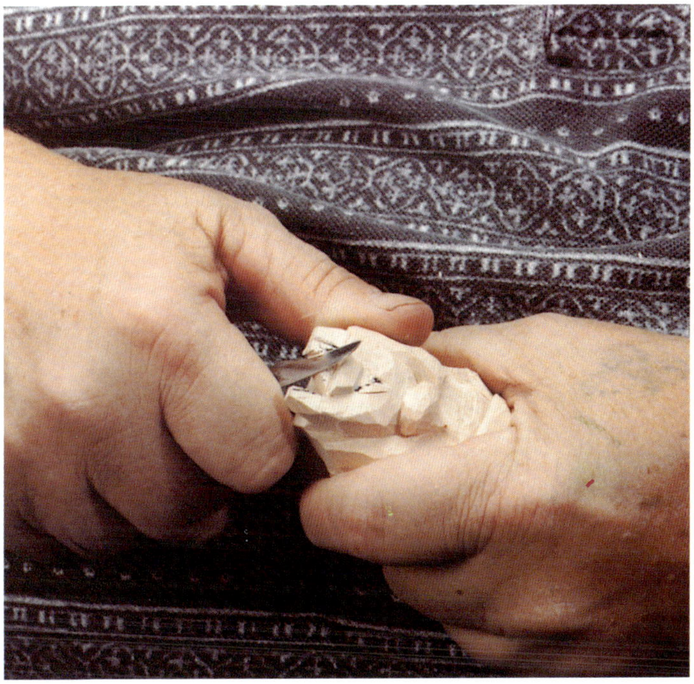

Cleaning out the area between the moustaches.

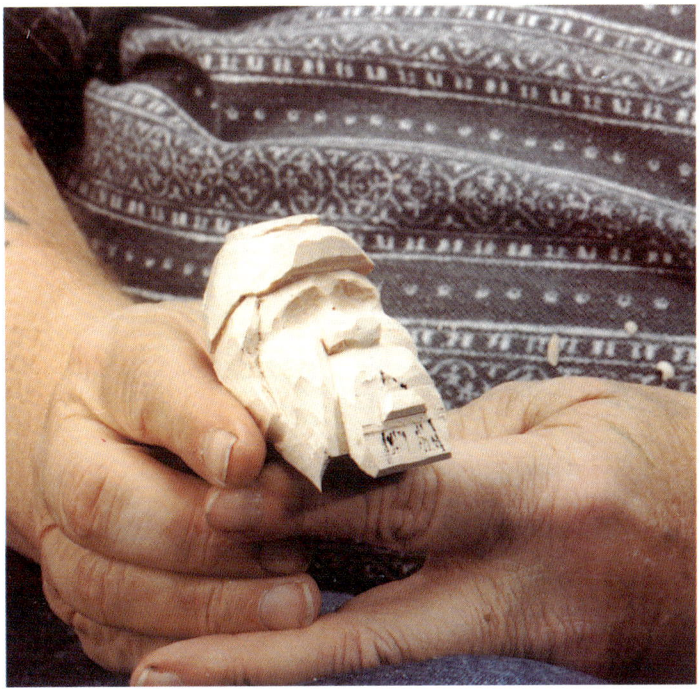

I cut down the moustache first to bring the chin out.

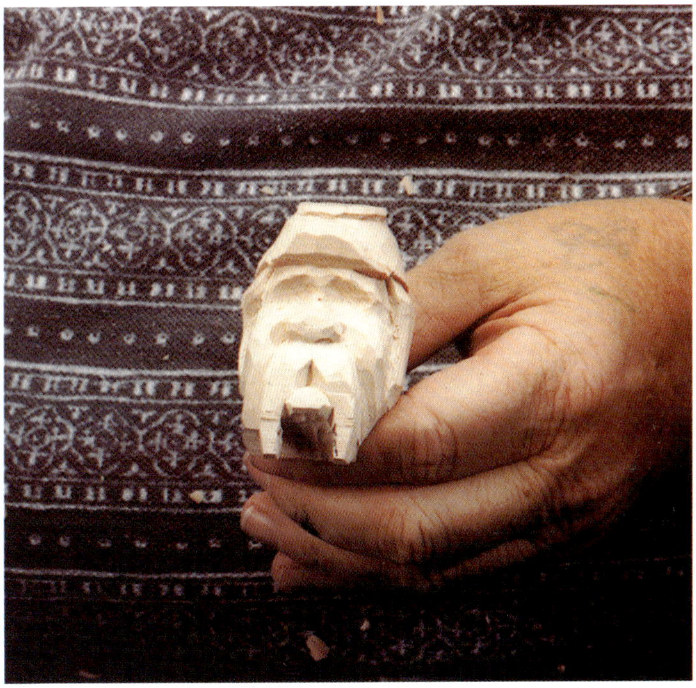

Progress.

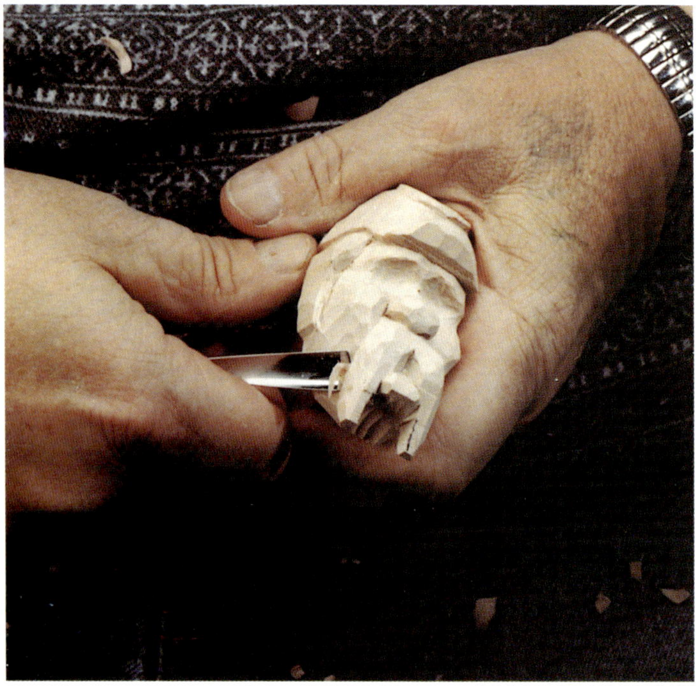

The jaw still looks heavy, so I'm bringing it up from the bottom.

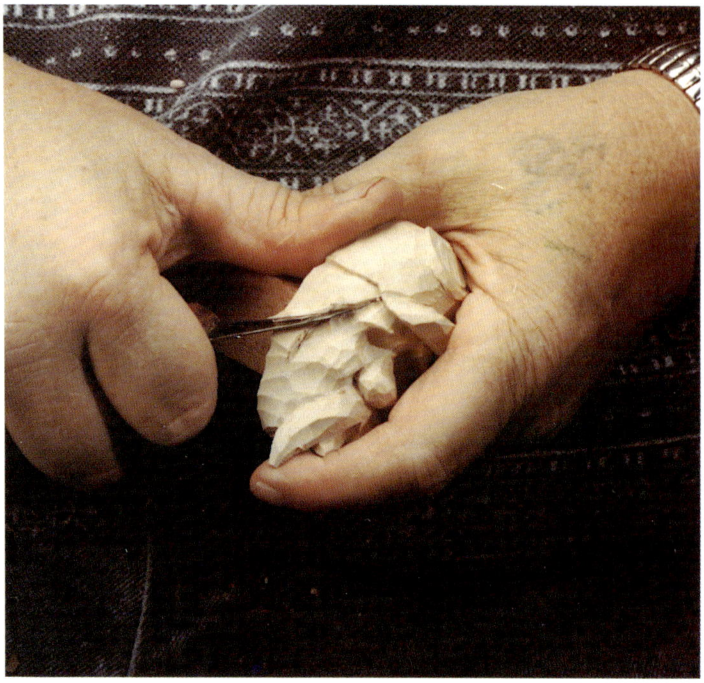

Now I'm taking some off the sideburn to bring out the hair.

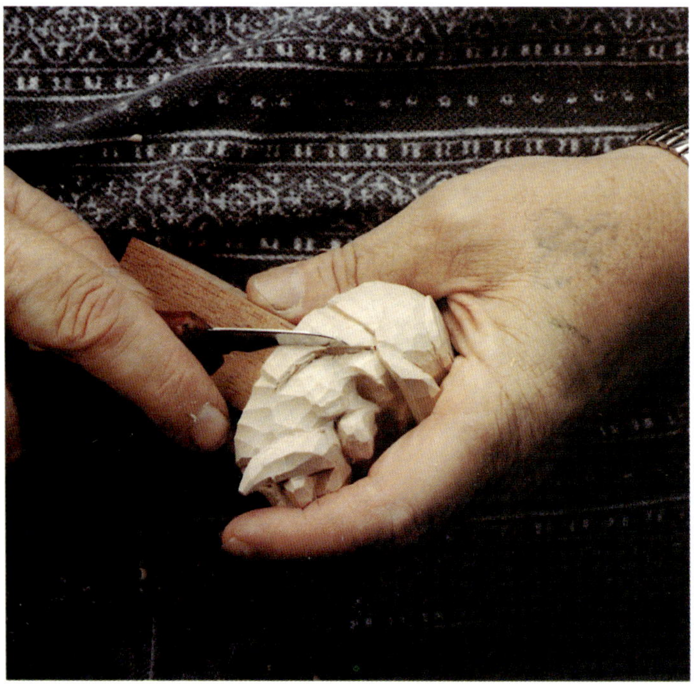

I'm making a stop cut to separate the hairline from the sideburn.

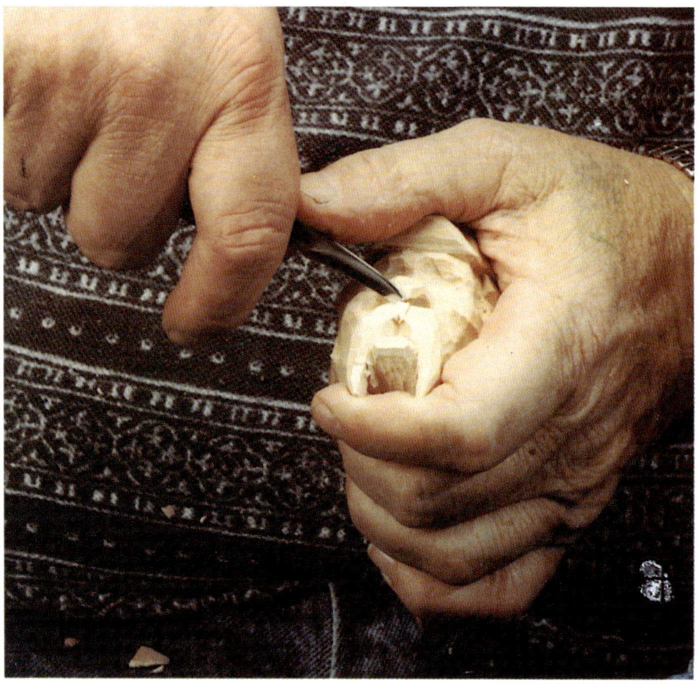

With three cuts of the knife, I poked out a triangle to separate the two moustaches under the nose.

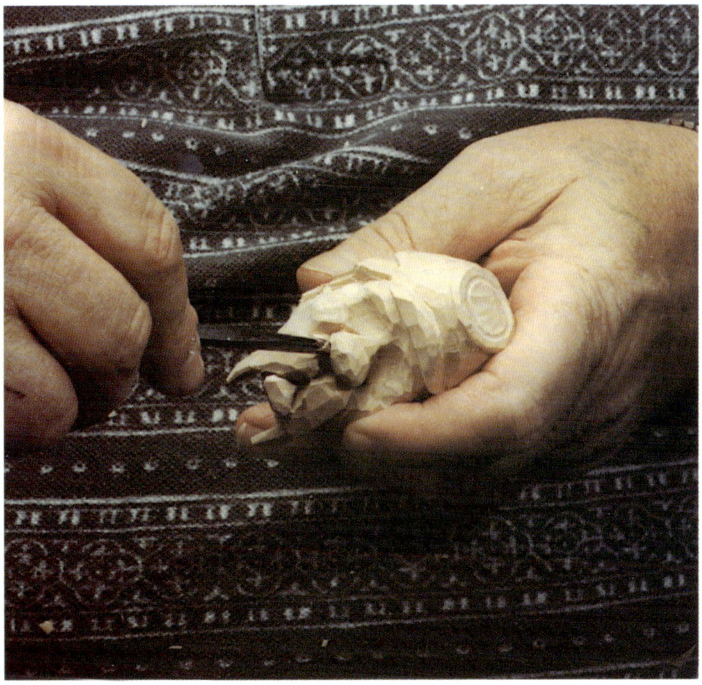

With a small half round, I'm punching out the nostrils.

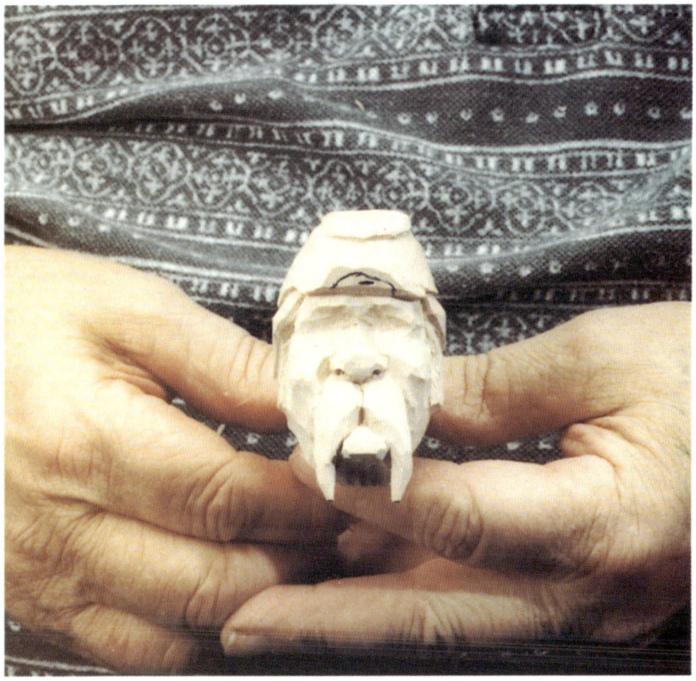

Progress. I'm marking the bill to make an undercut.

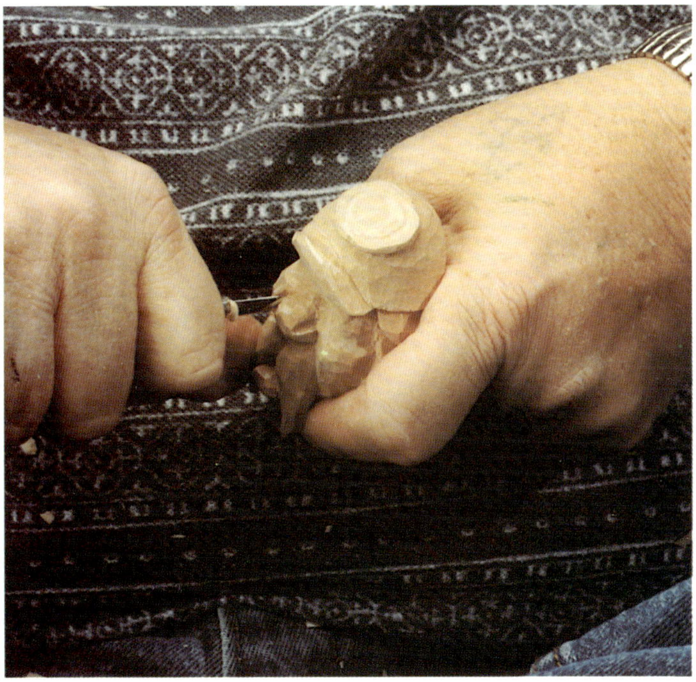

You can use the same tool to define the flange around the nostril.

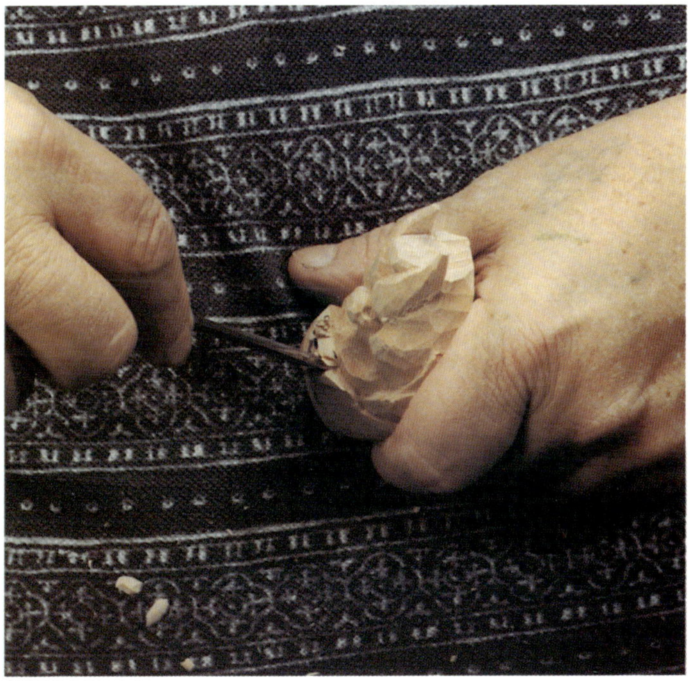

Be careful not to break the bill off! It's better to come straight in at an angle, instead of prying in an upward motion.

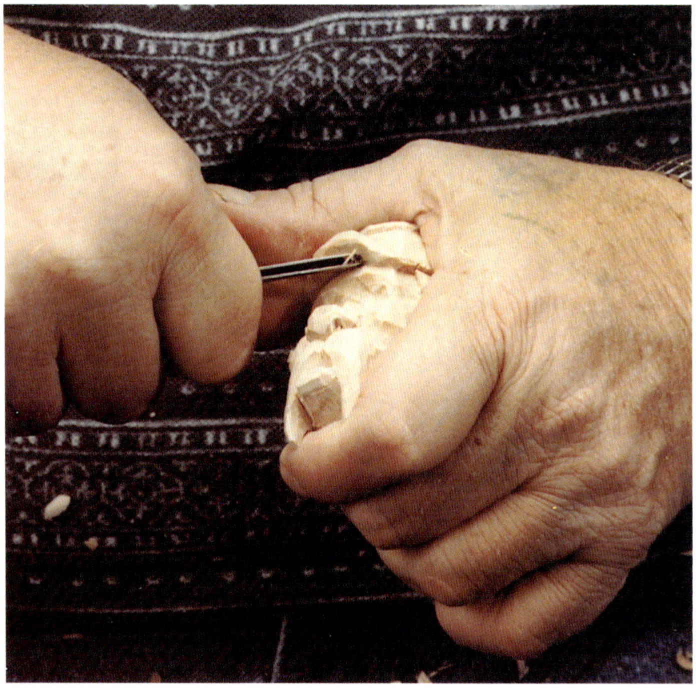

Use the small V-tool to clean it up.

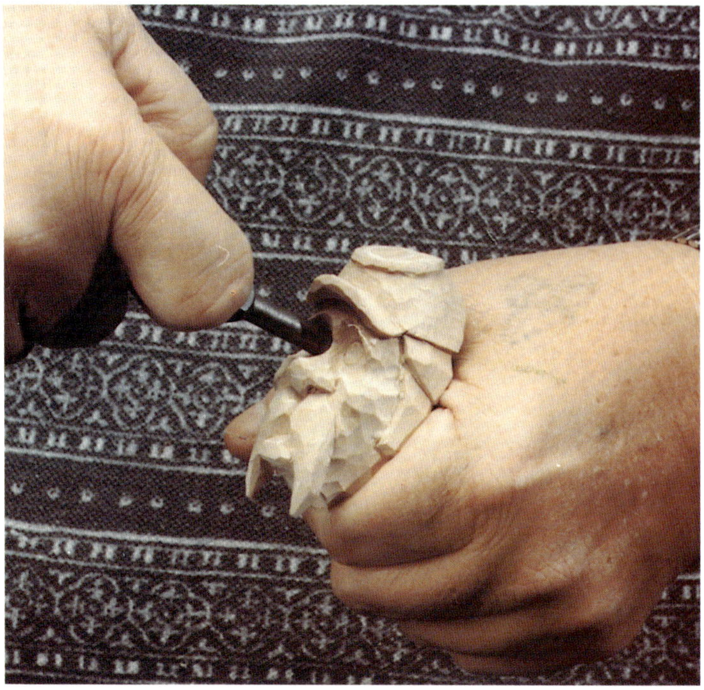

I think he needs some googly eyes. I'm using a pretty big, round eyepunch here. Just ram it in and rotate.

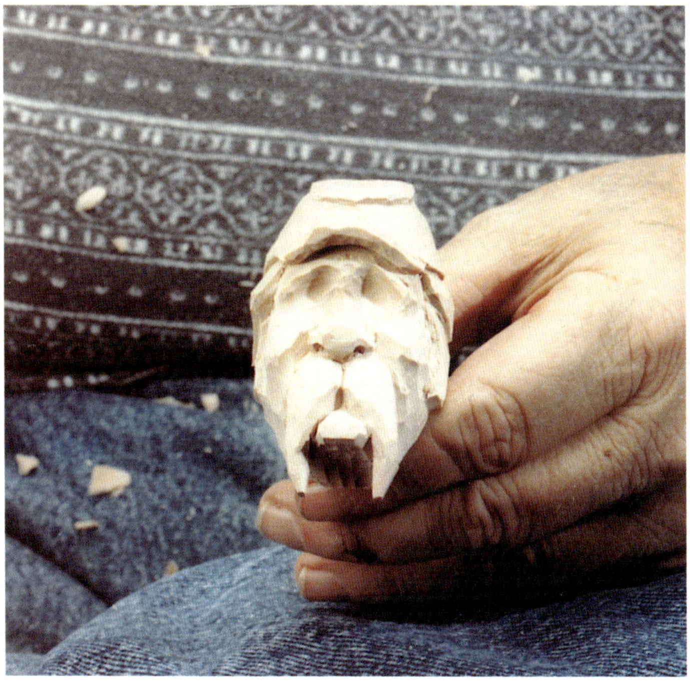

I raised the eyebrows using the half round gouge.

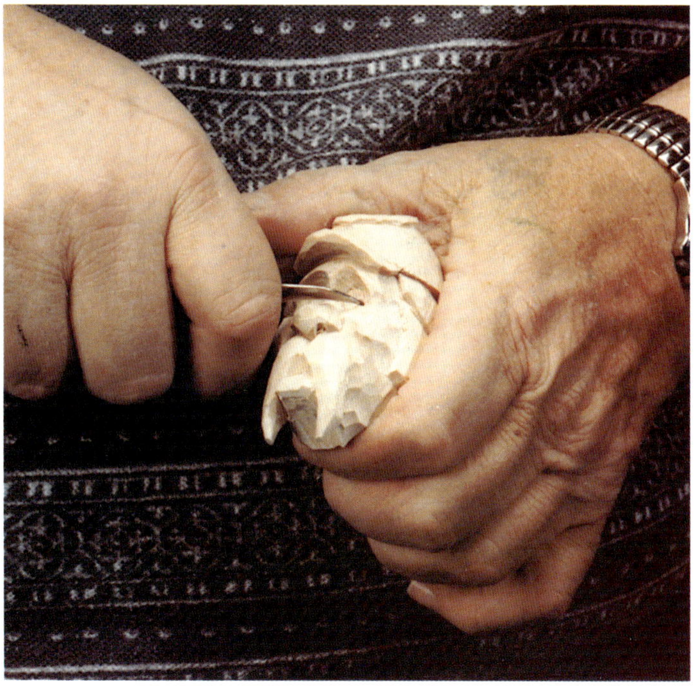

Make three little cuts in a triangle to bring out the corner of each eye.

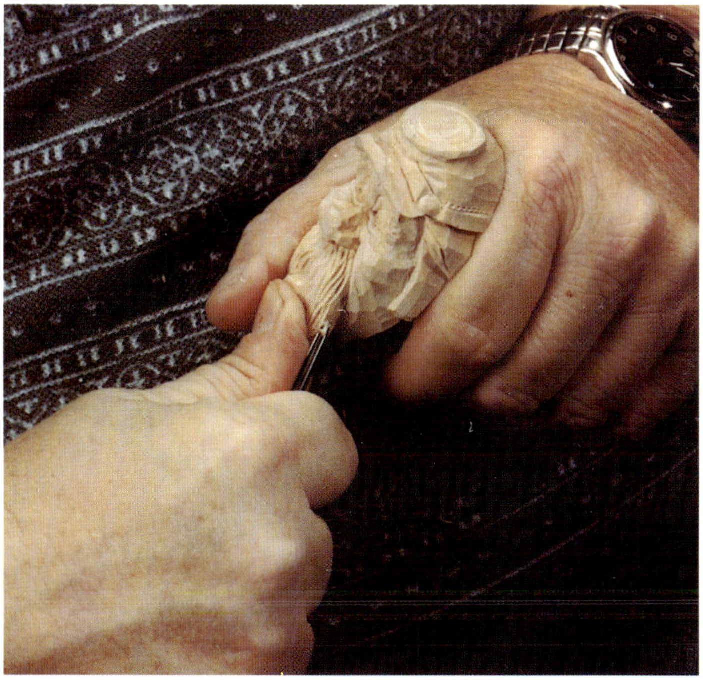

The veiner makes good hair texture. I'm starting with the moustache.

The finished piece.

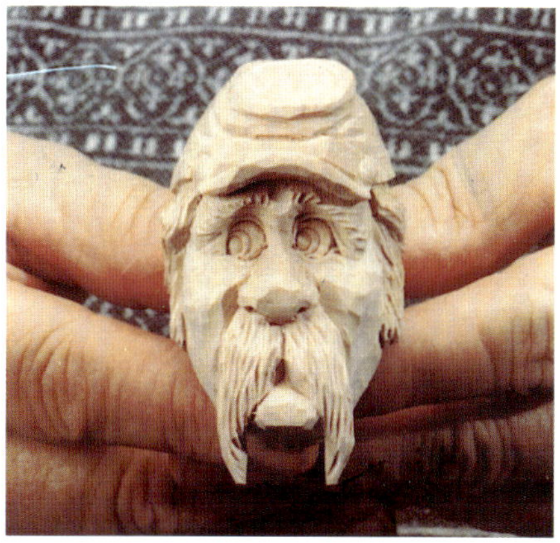

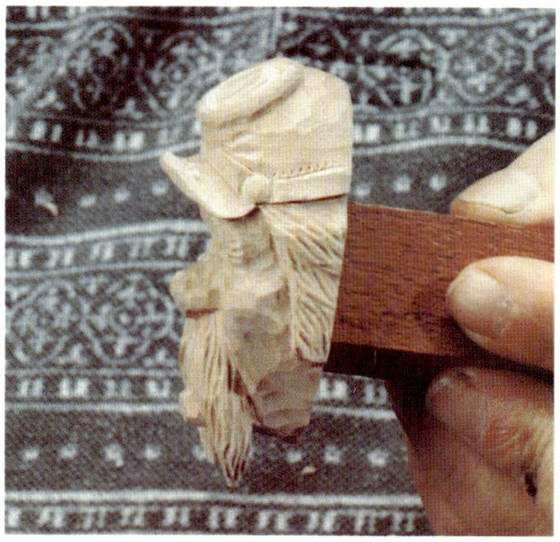

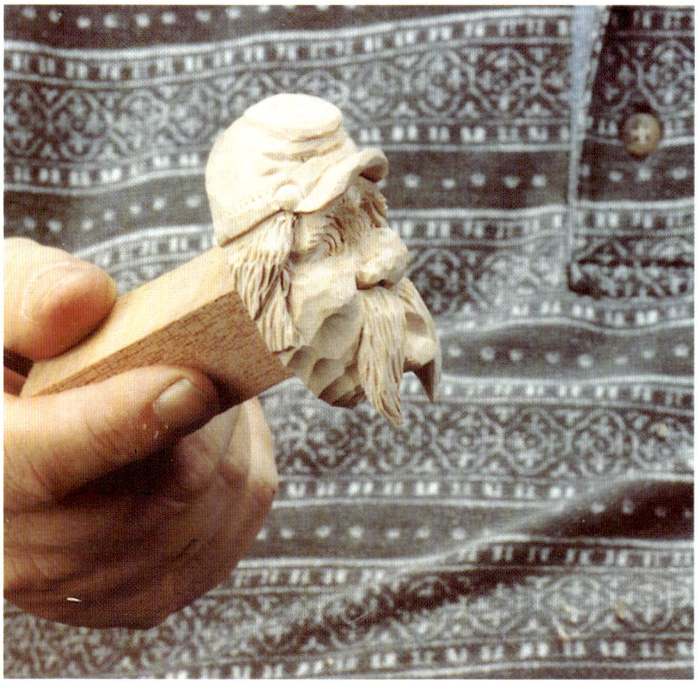

Hair.

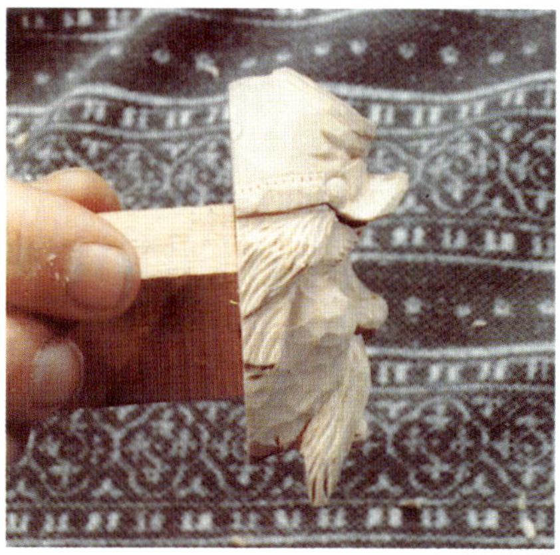

Painting & Finishing The Projects

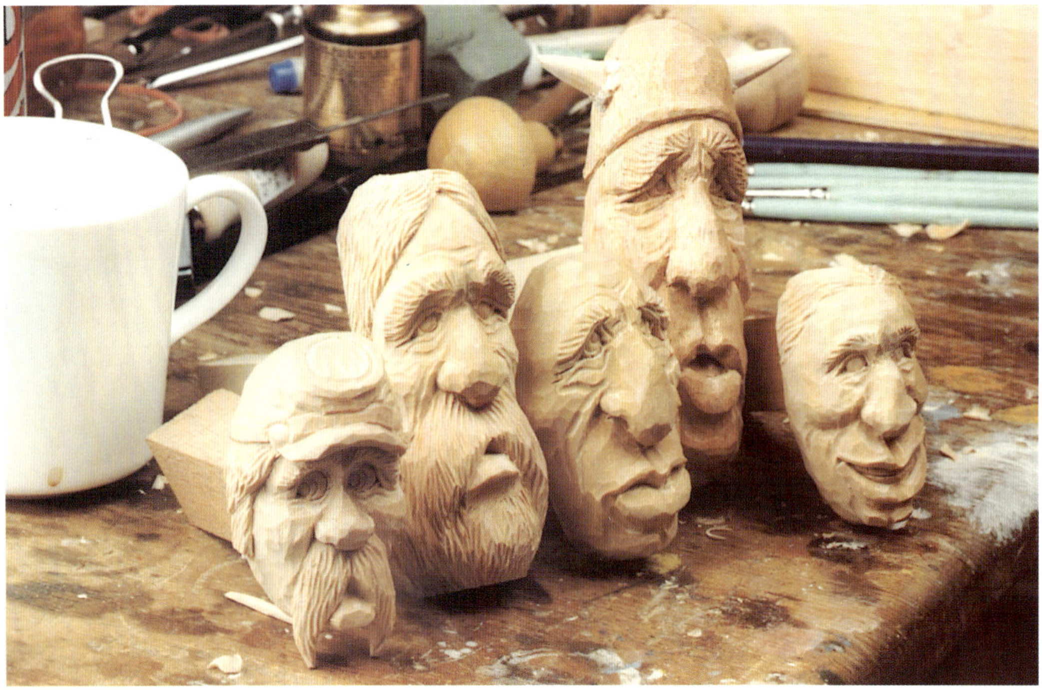

Now we'll paint, using artist's oil colors. You can use acrylic paint if you'd rather, using water instead of turpentine. I'll start with the flesh colors. Since I'm painting five different faces, I'll play around with the shades to get some variety. My standard flesh tone is half white, a quarter raw siena, and a quarter of "flesh" color. Mix with plenty of turpentine.

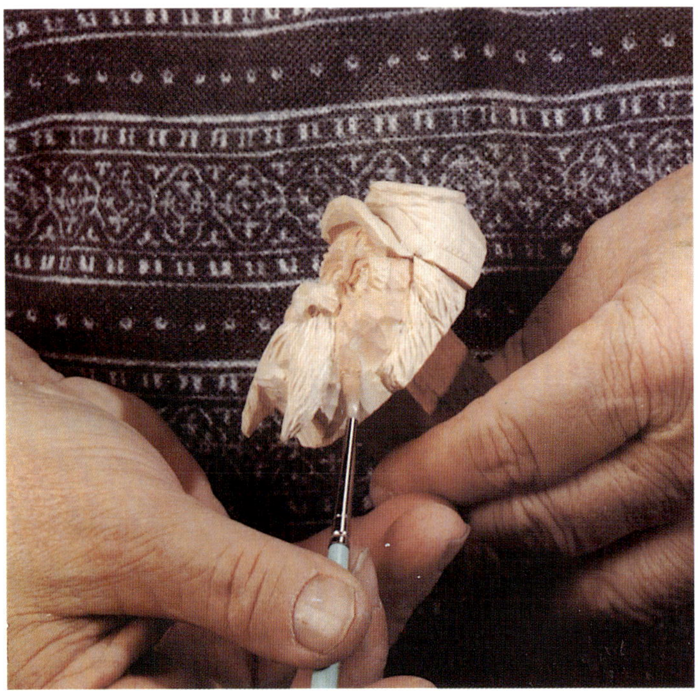

I would like the soldier to have a scottish look, with red hair. That means I need a fair pinkish shade for his skin.

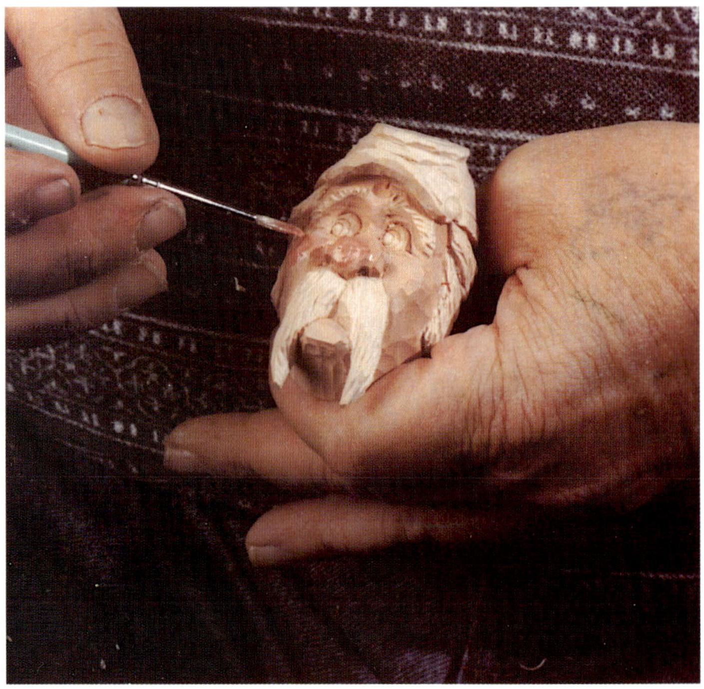

Blend in some red for a blush.

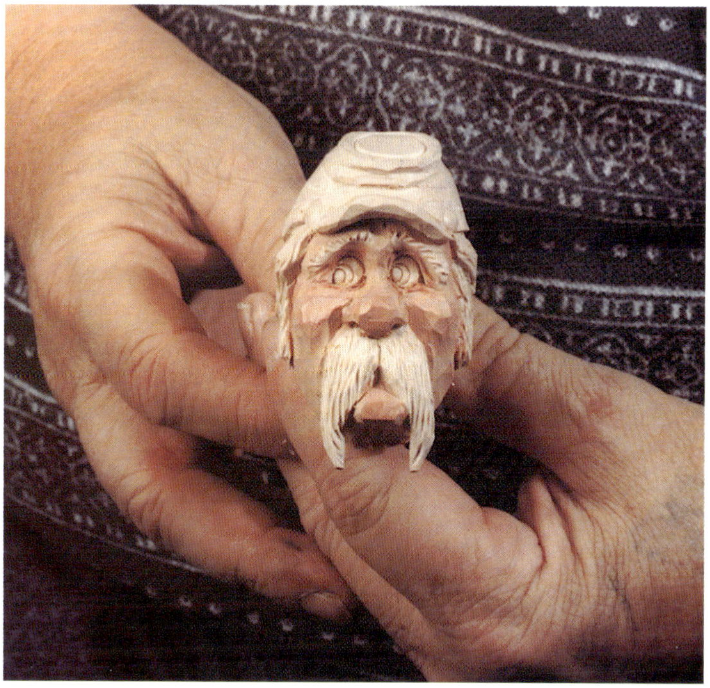

Progress.

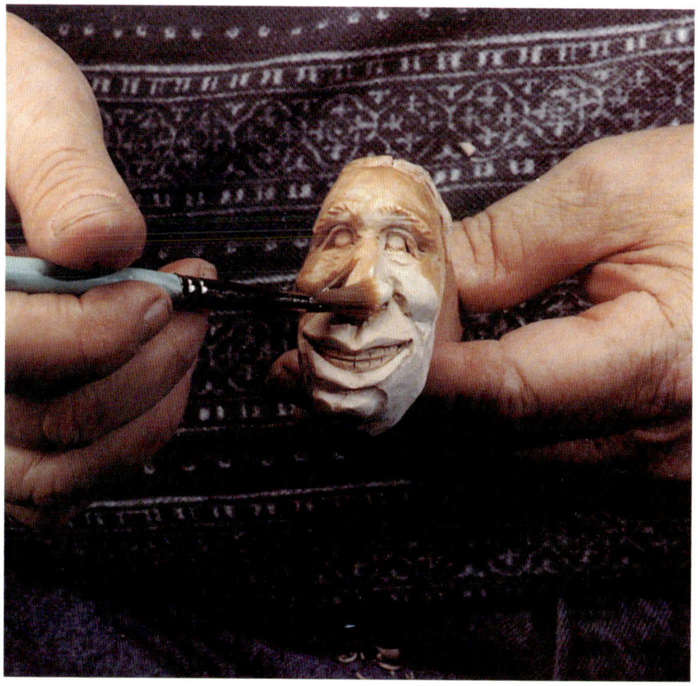

Sometimes I like to use an undercoat of boiled linseed oil, which brings out the color of the paint.

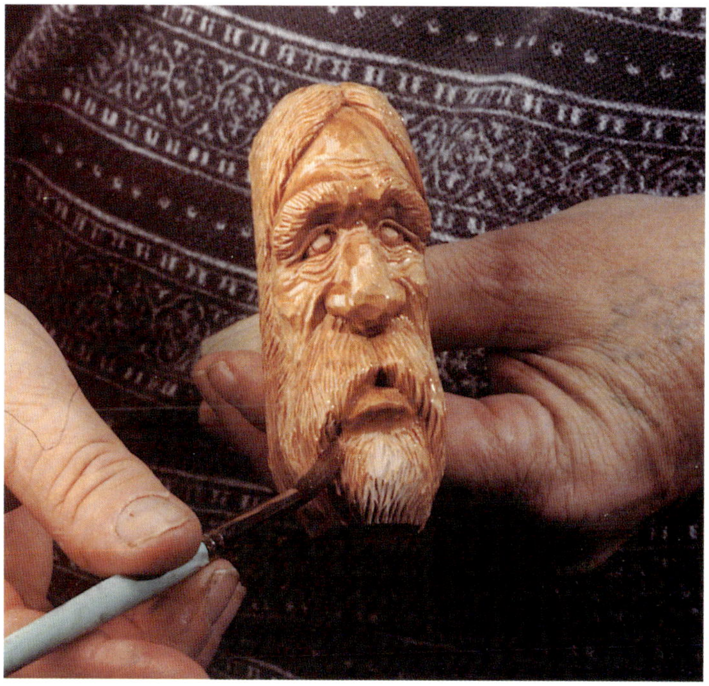

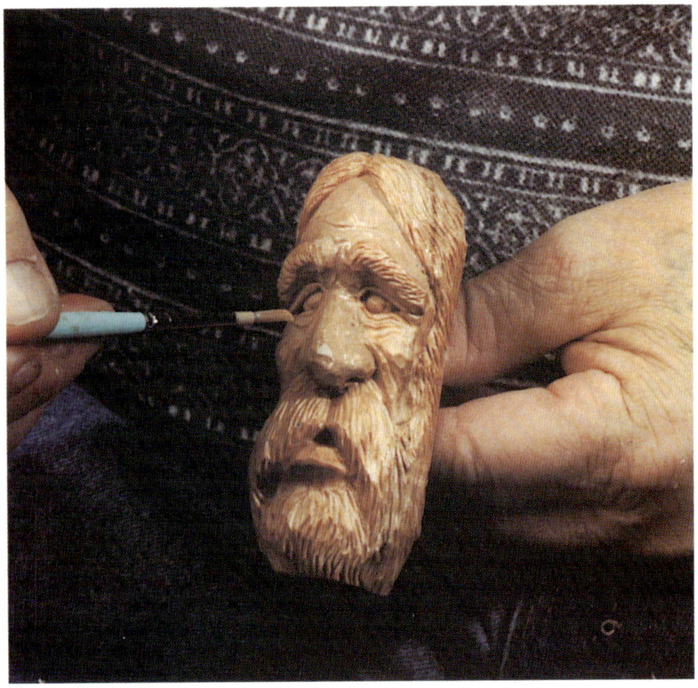

I mixed the paint for this face with a little less red and a little more siena. The color of the wood also has a lot to do with the way the paint comes out.

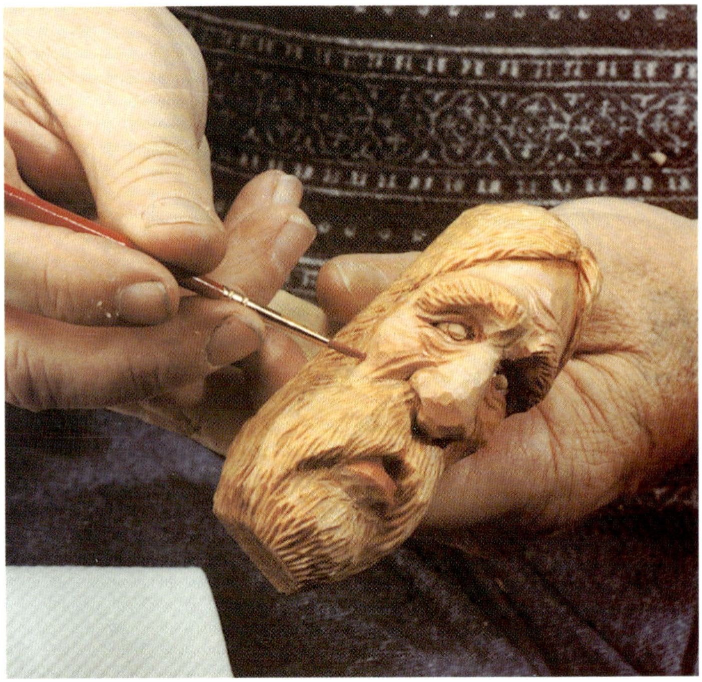

A little burnt siena adds shading.

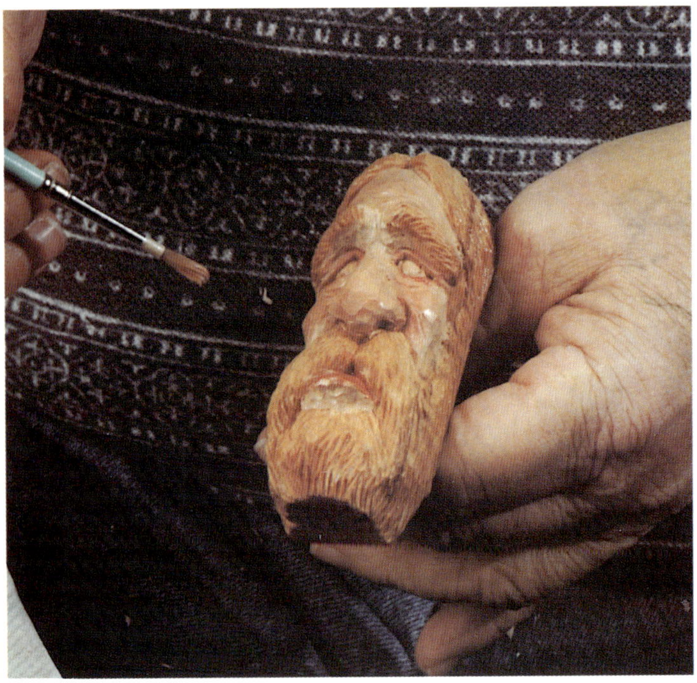

I added some red on the cheeks and lips, and I'm using a dry brush to blend it.

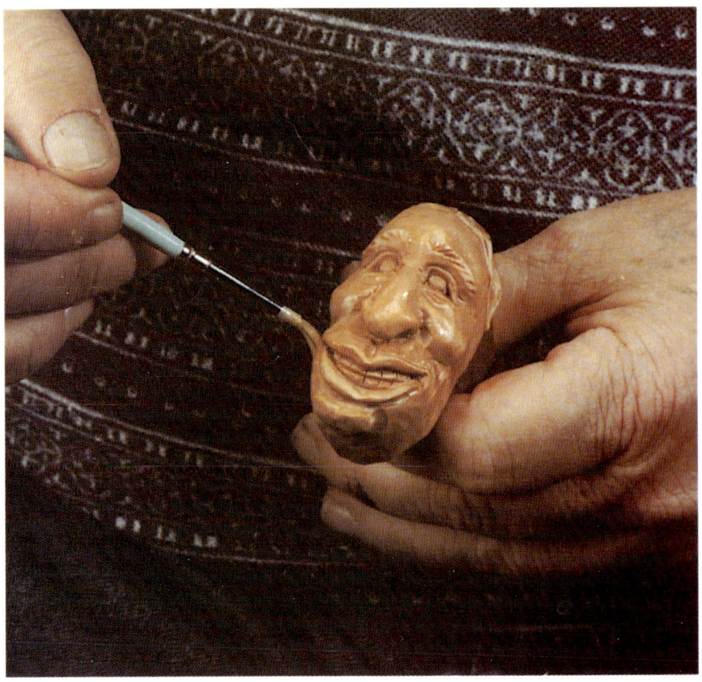

This flesh tone has both raw and burnt siena in it. It makes an interesting olive mediterranean color.

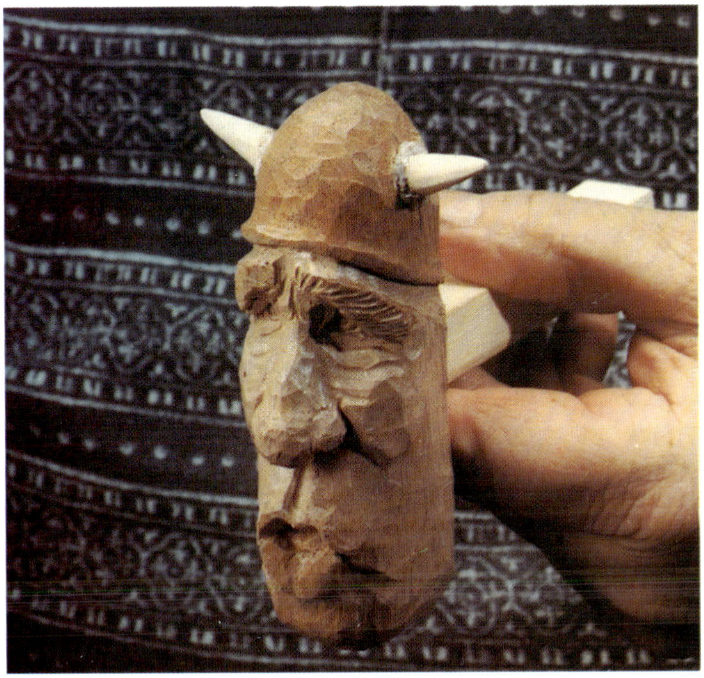

The viking should be have a pinker tone, especially with that dark mahogany under there. Notice how well the super and wood glues worked together for the horns; it looks very realistic.

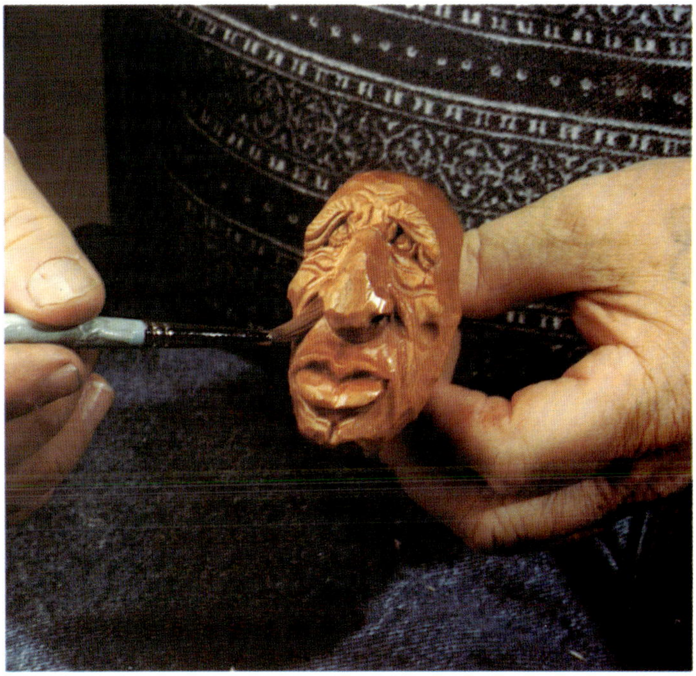

I'll try burnt siena by itself for this one.

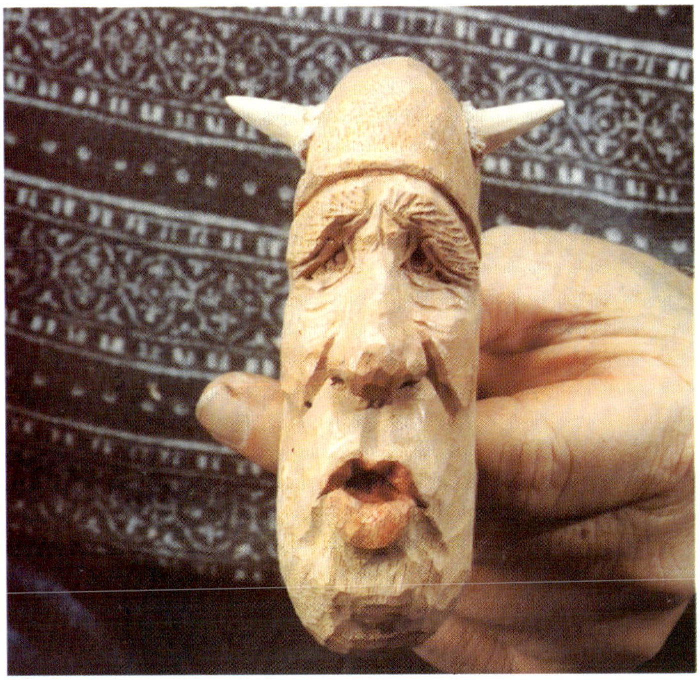

Progress. I've added the red for lips and blush.

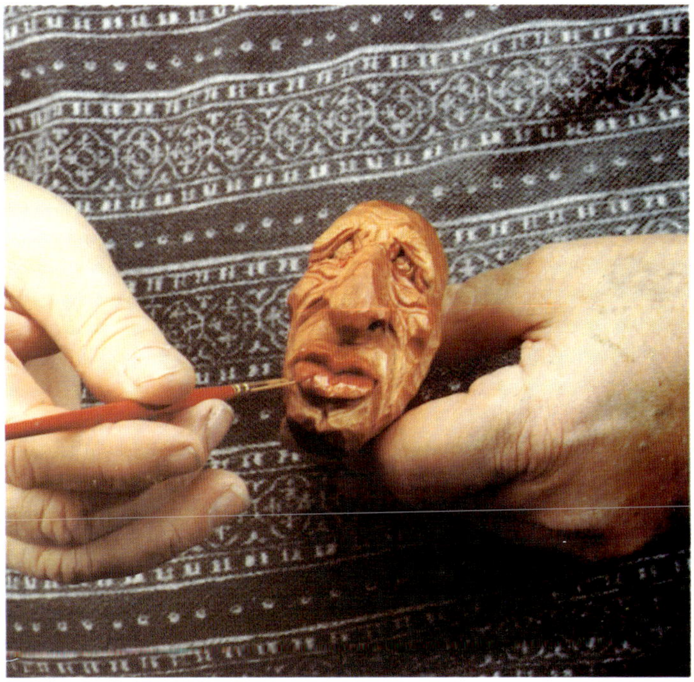

The red blending looks good here.

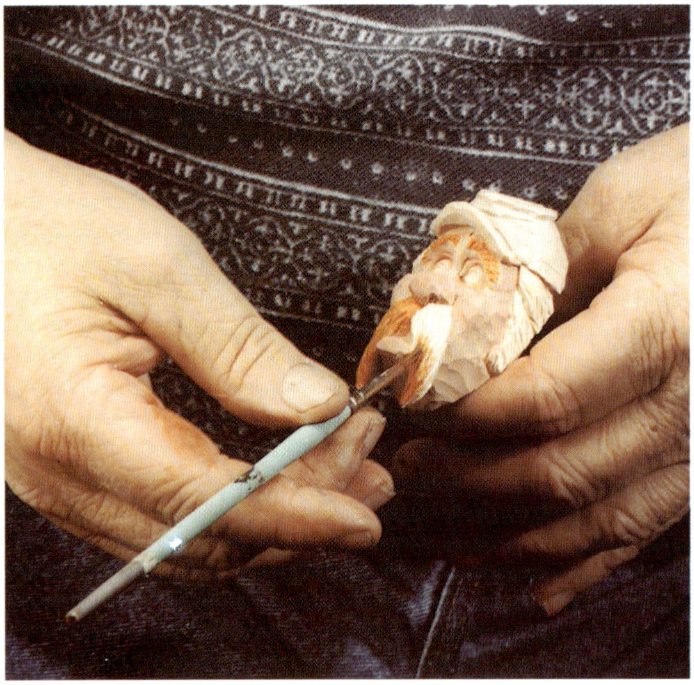

I'm using a bright orange for the rebel's hair.

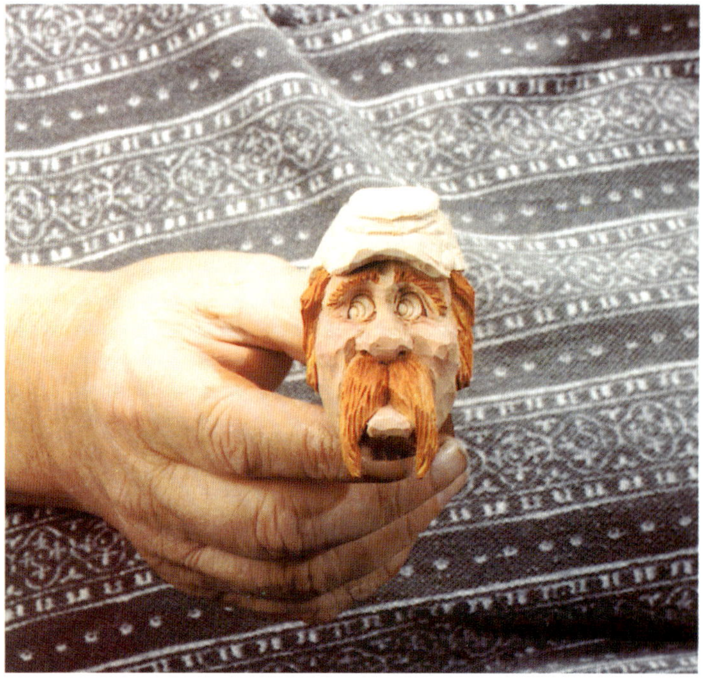

I blended some yellow on the ends to finish it nicely.

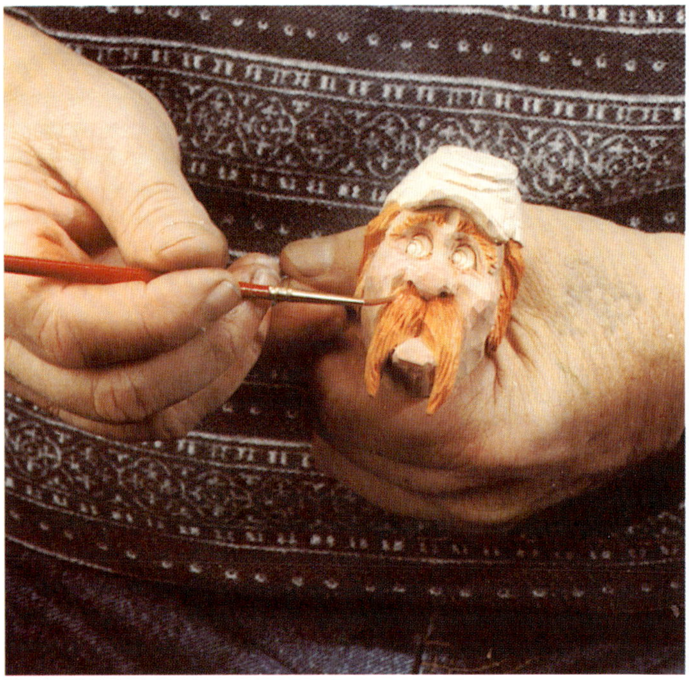

Make the roots a little darker. I'm using burnt siena. Another point to remember is that no matter what color the hair, the eyebrows will always be a little darker.

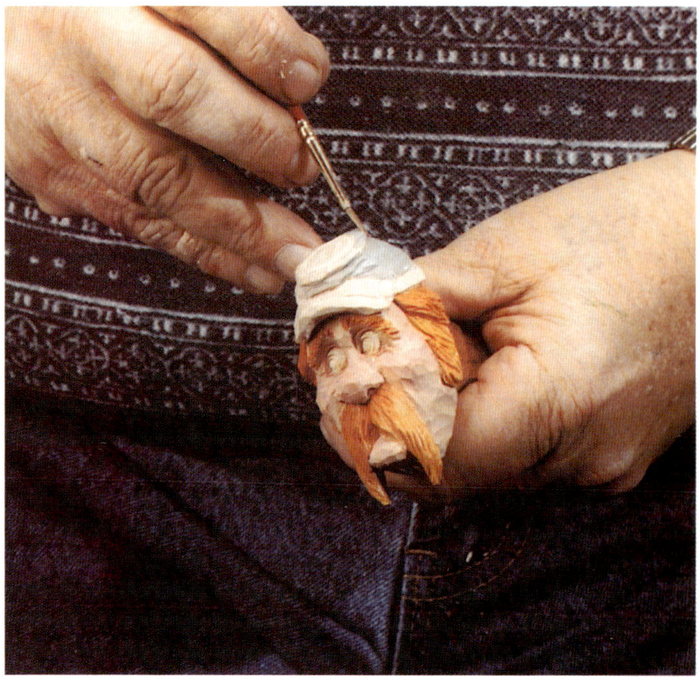

The hat, of course, needs to be gray.

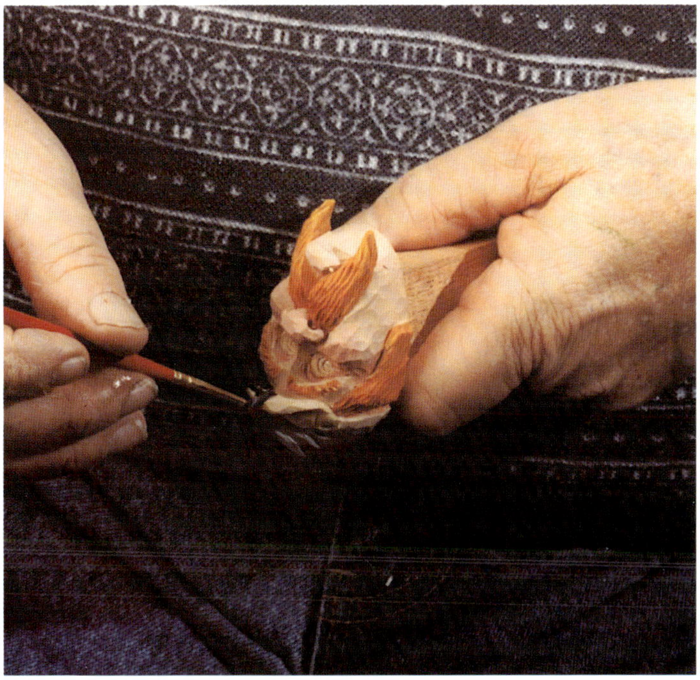

When you're painting the brim of a hat, it's best to start from underneath because it loads up the fiber and acts as a barrier for any paint that might drip from the top onto the face. I'm using black.

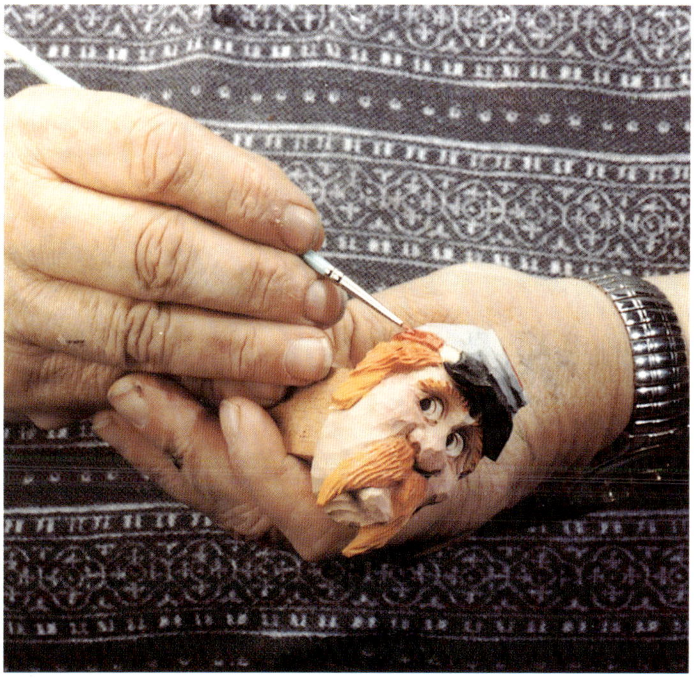

I've decided he looks like an artilleryman, so I'll paint that band red.

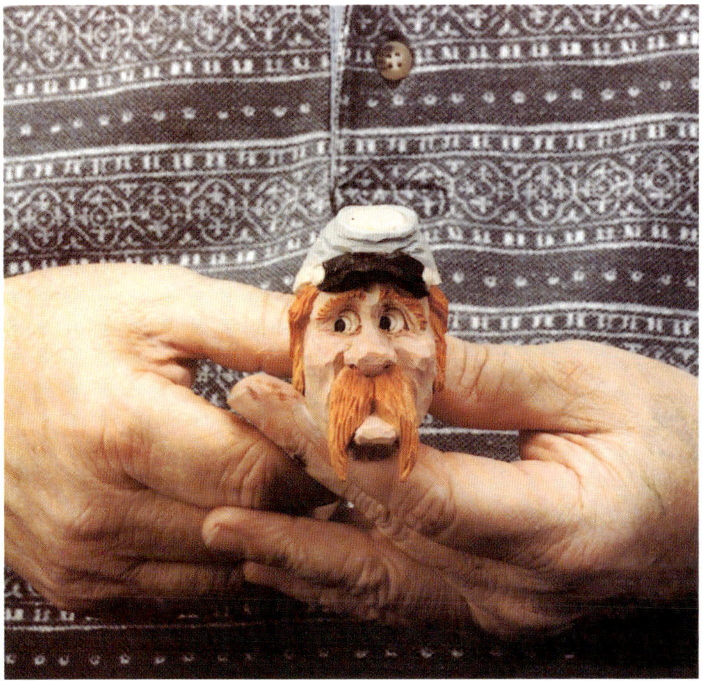

Progress.

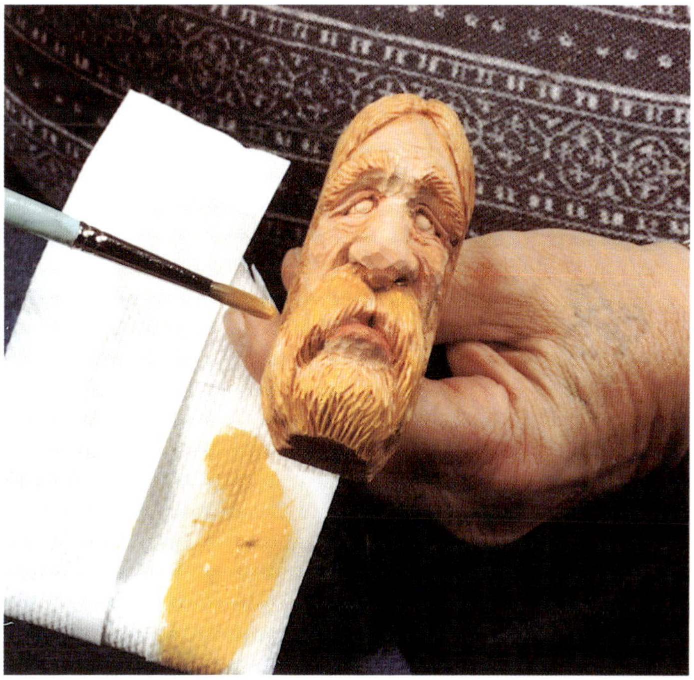

A bit of yellow here blends in nicely with the wood and the texture.

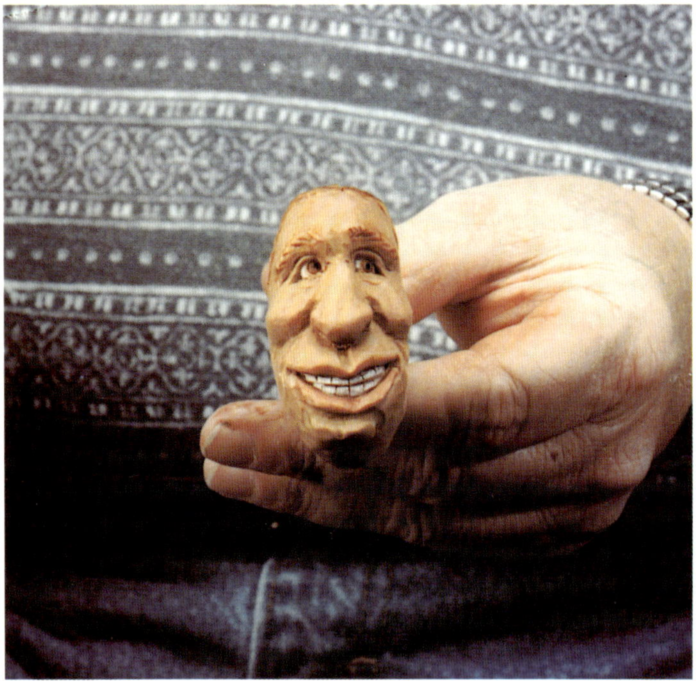

Some white here brings the smile right out!

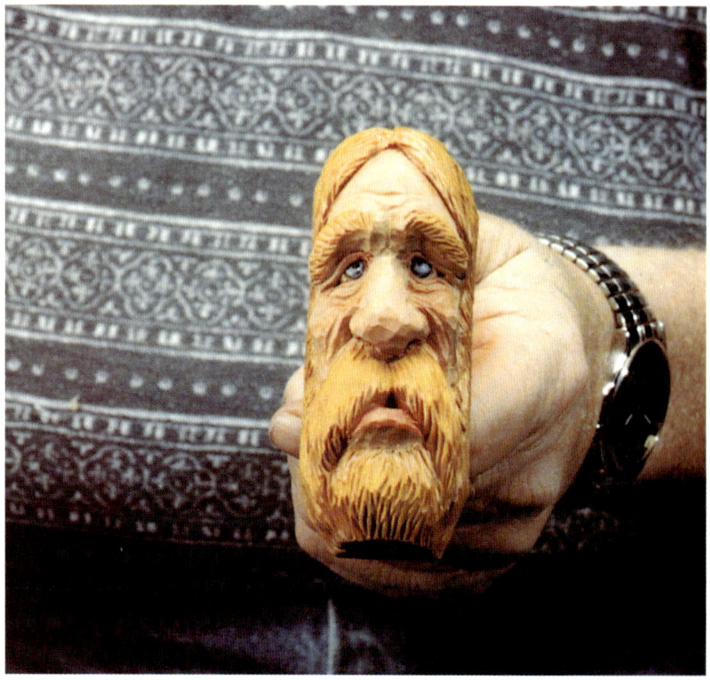

A tiny dot of white can bring an eye to life.

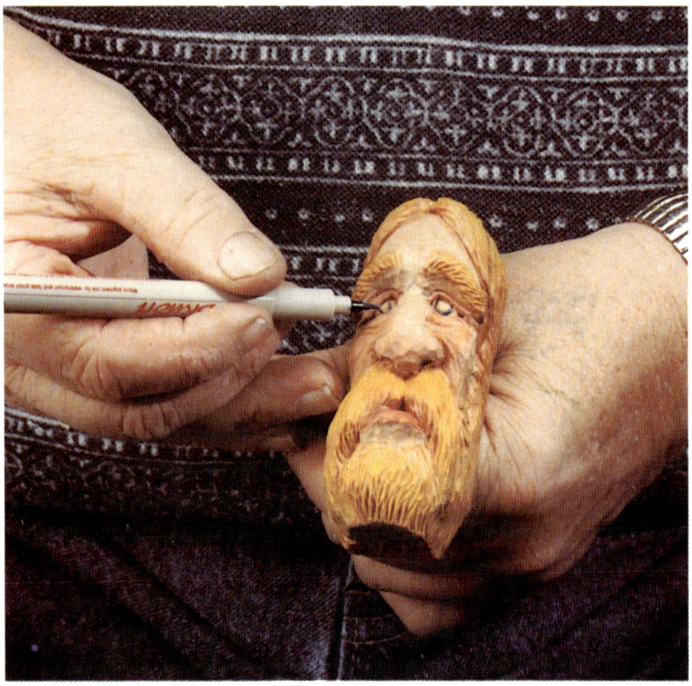

A brush pen can be helpful for small details like the irises.

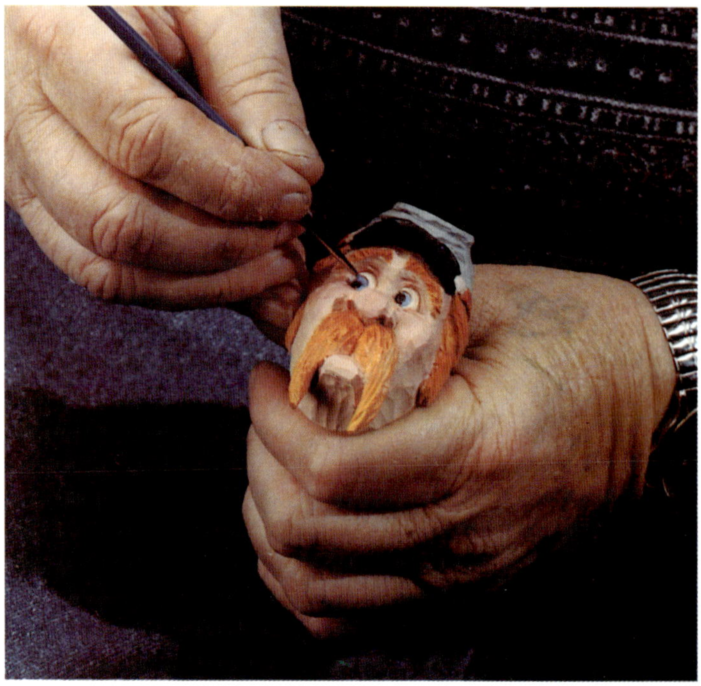

You can also paint the iris on.

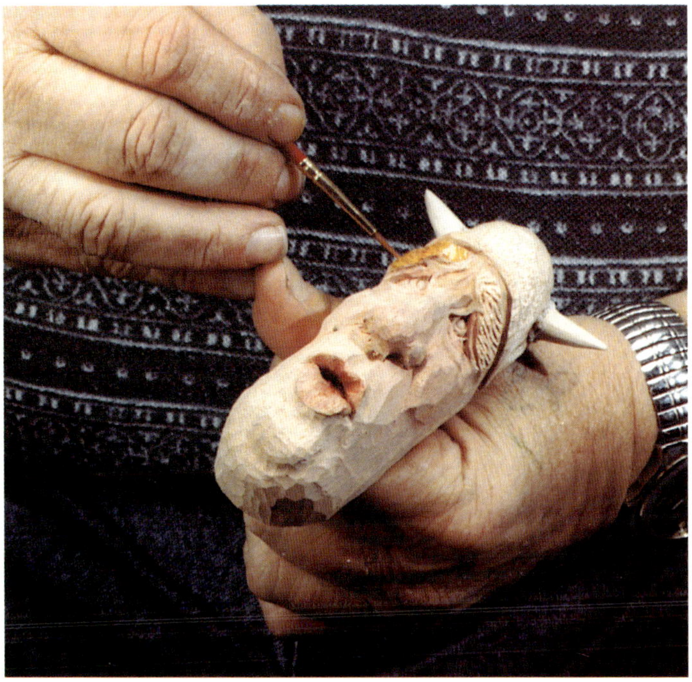

The viking will be blonde. If we added a thick braid on either side, we'd have an opera singer!

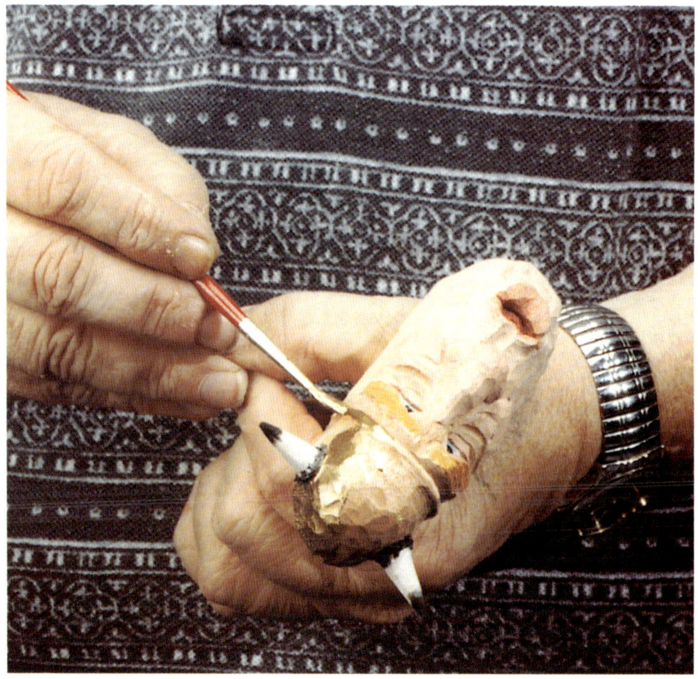

Gold leaf paint is perfect for the helmet.

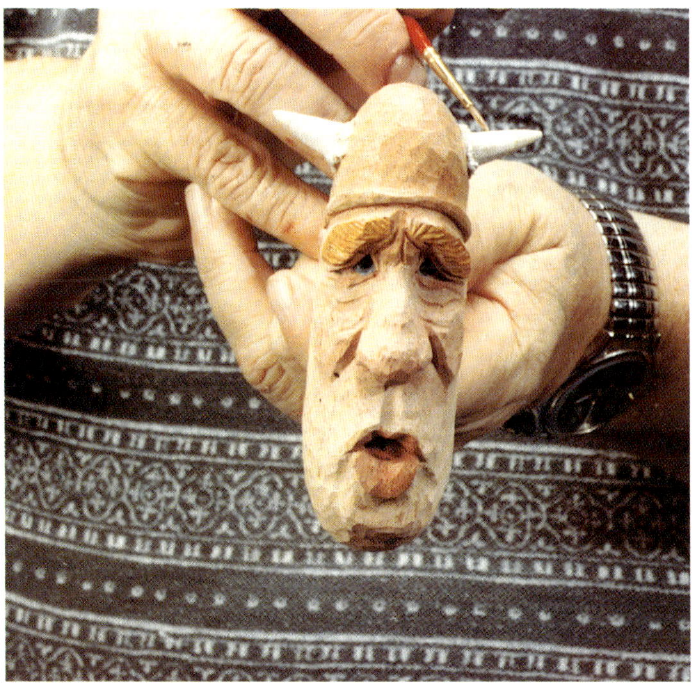

Finishing the horns.

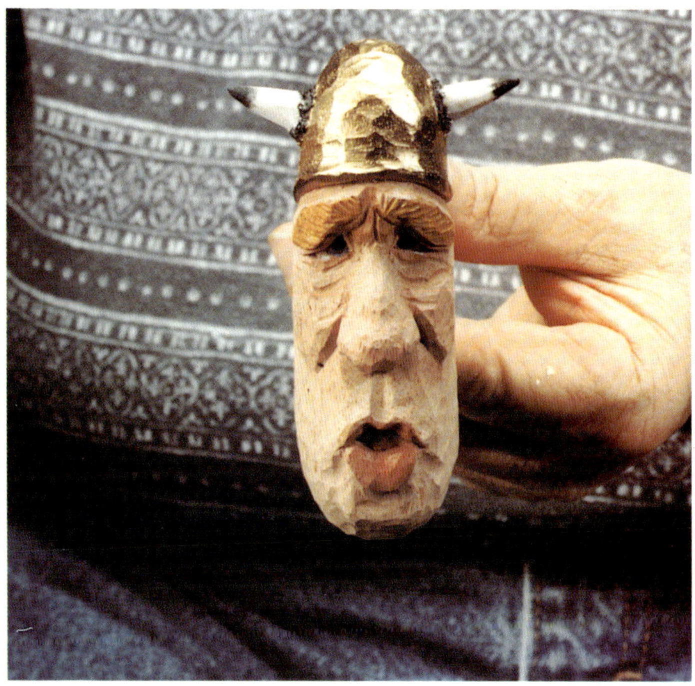

The finished viking.

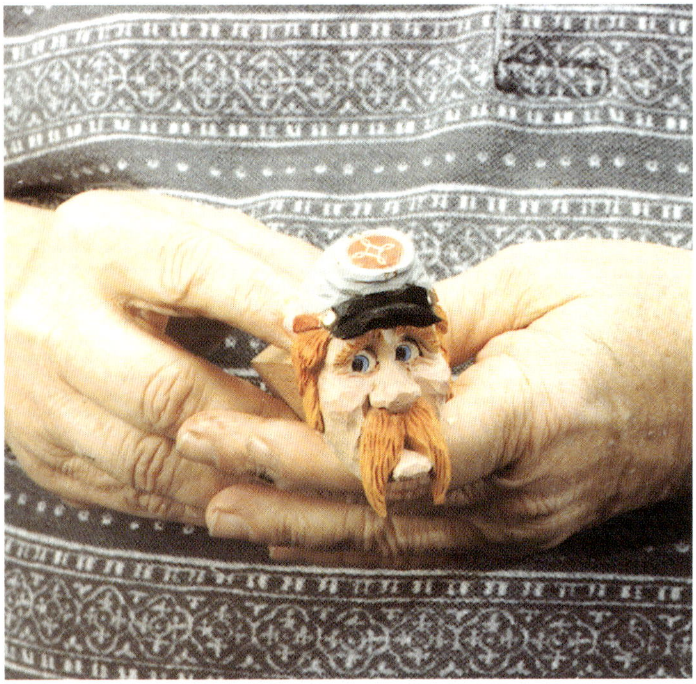

The gold leaf is also good for brass buttons and insignia, too.

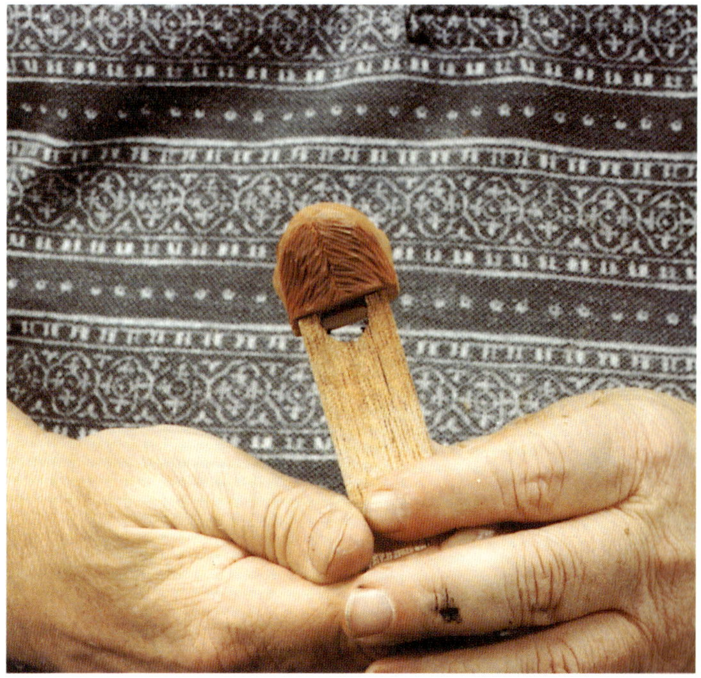

Remember, we made the laughing man for the neck hanger, with the hole in the handle.

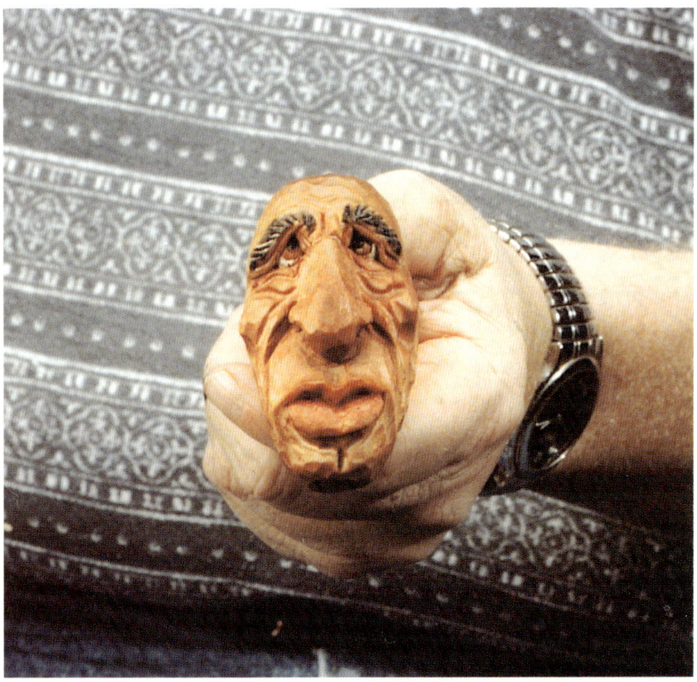

Black eyebrows give this fellow a whole new look!

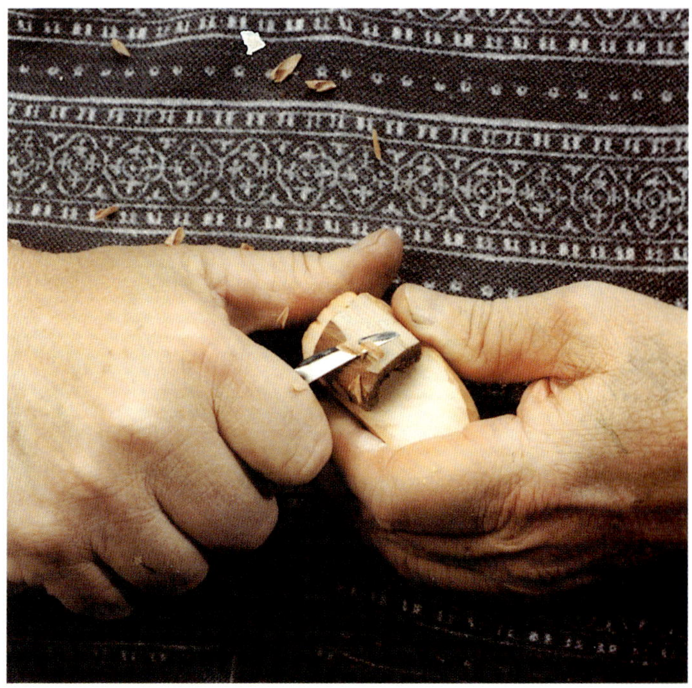

I've sawed off the excess handle. Now I'm rounding off the edges.

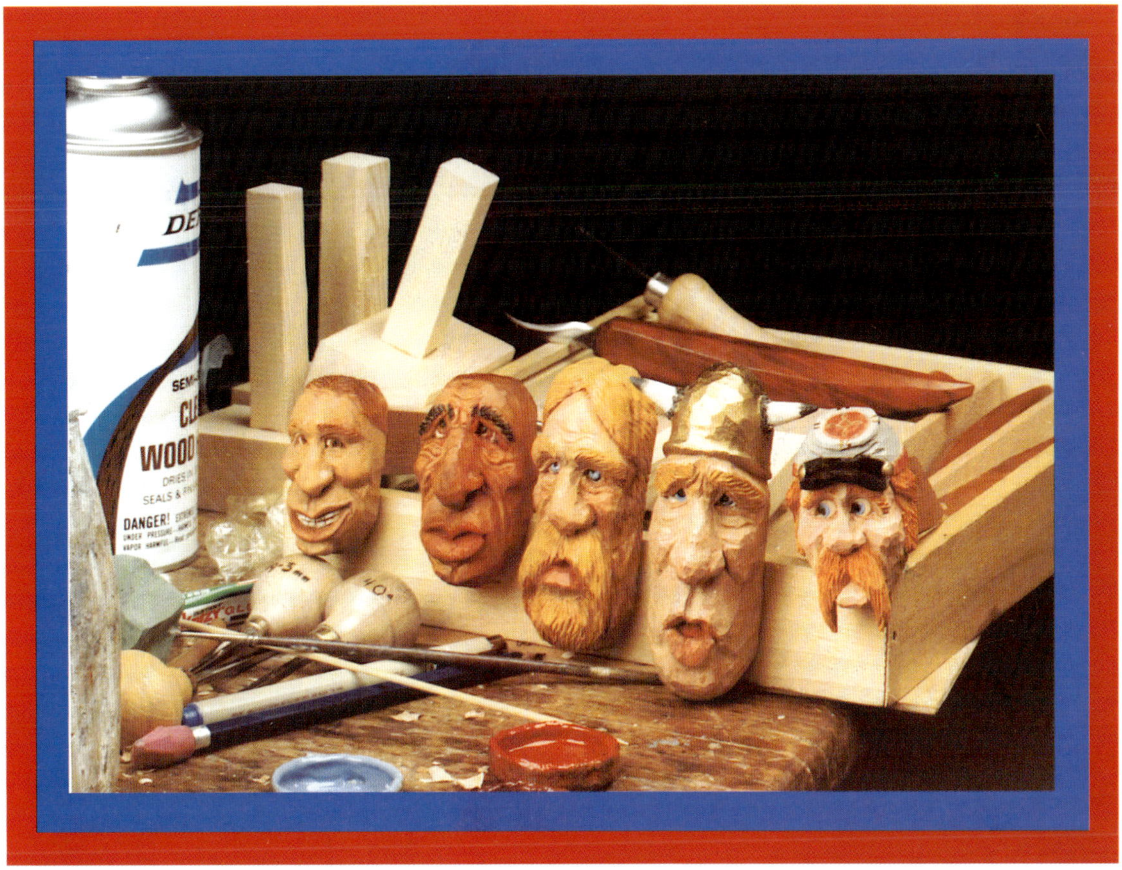

Finished Projects .

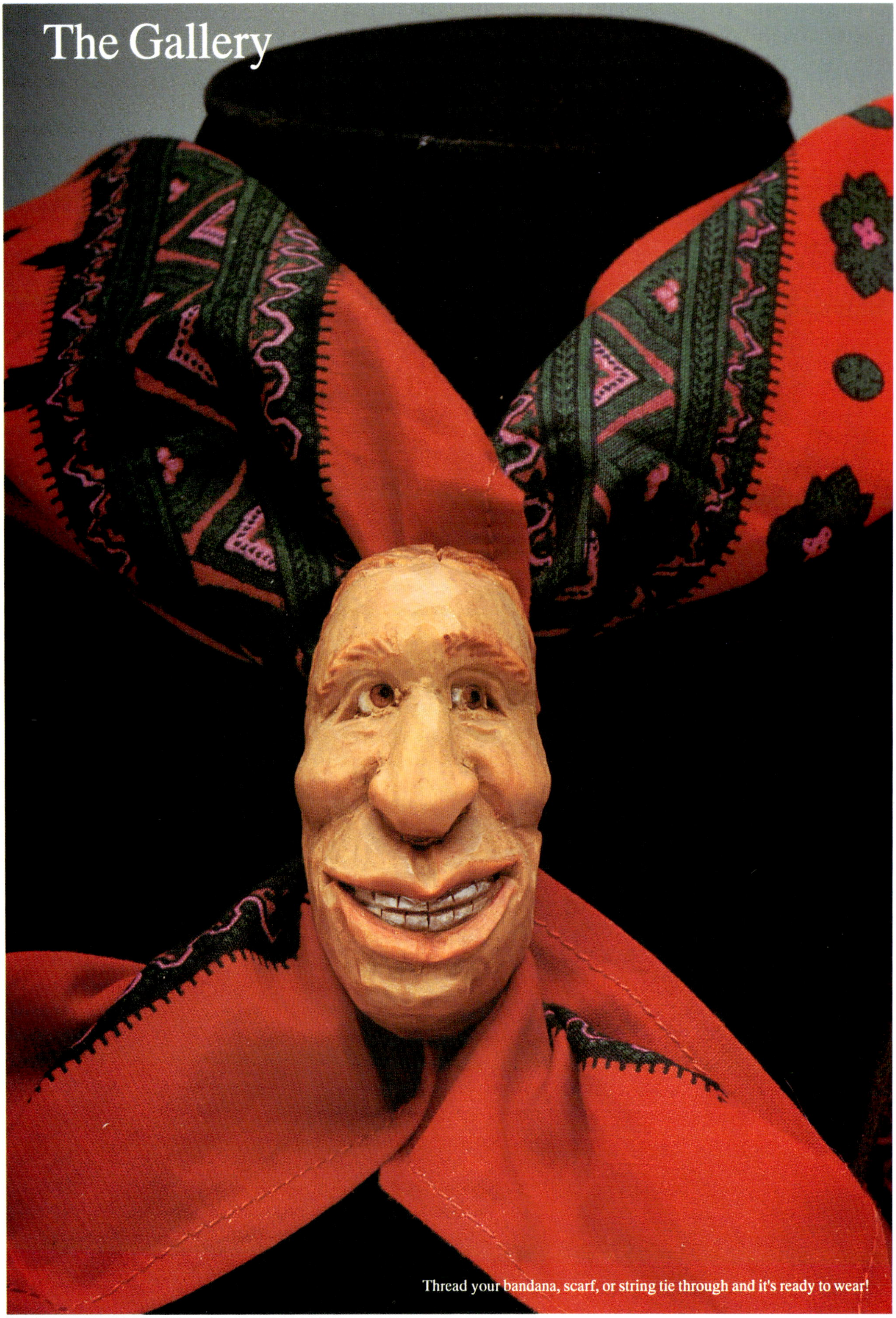

Thread your bandana, scarf, or string tie through and it's ready to wear!

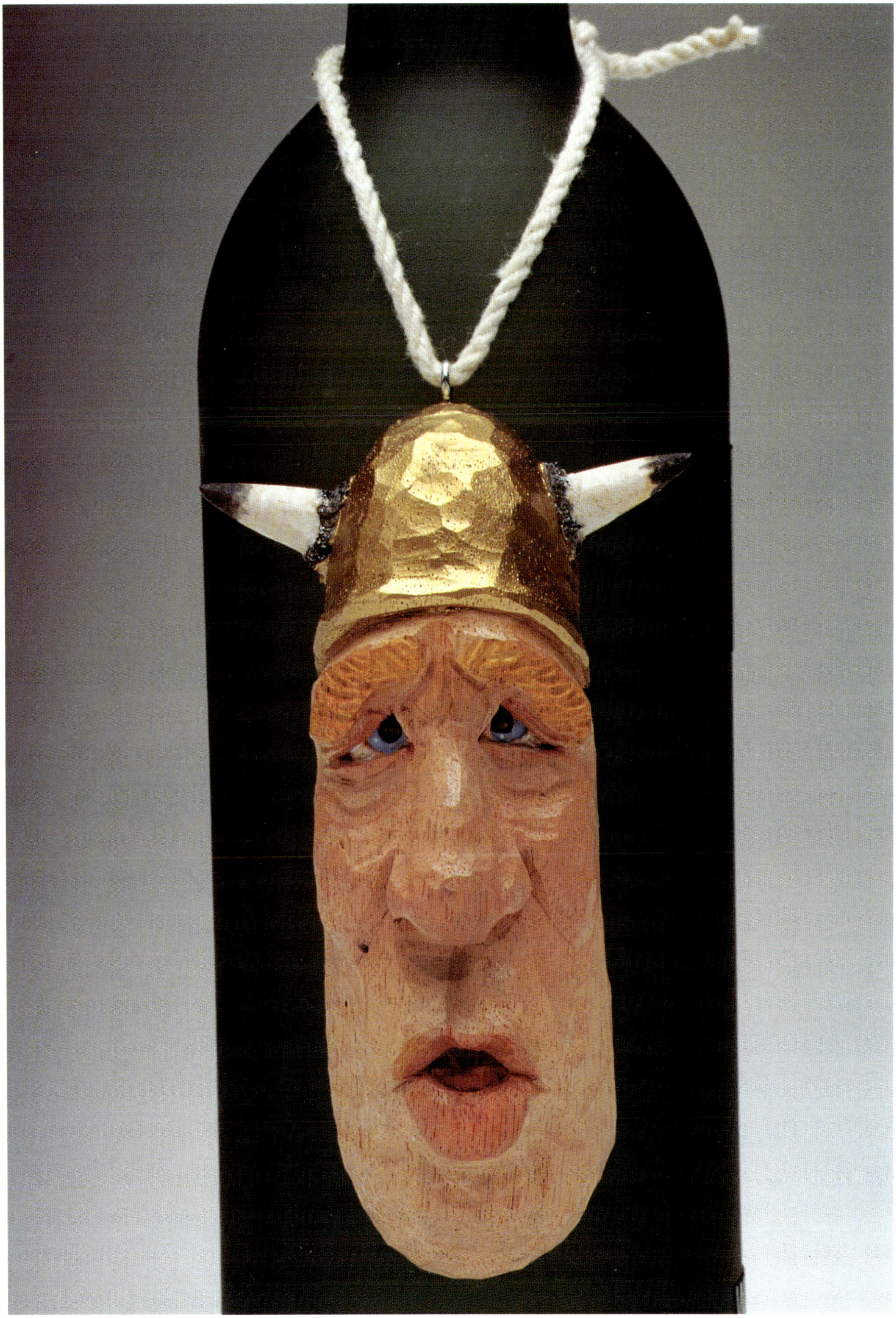

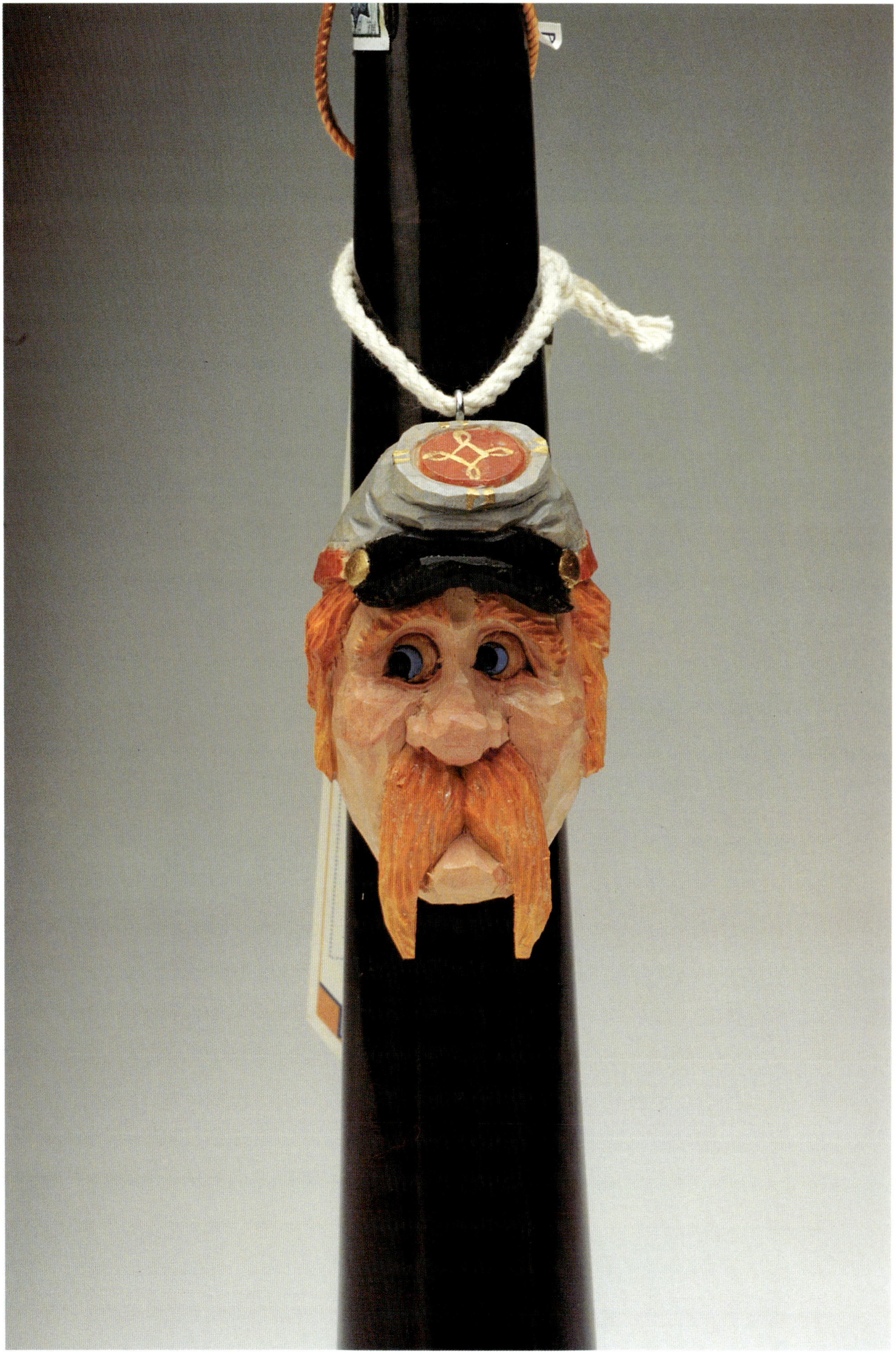

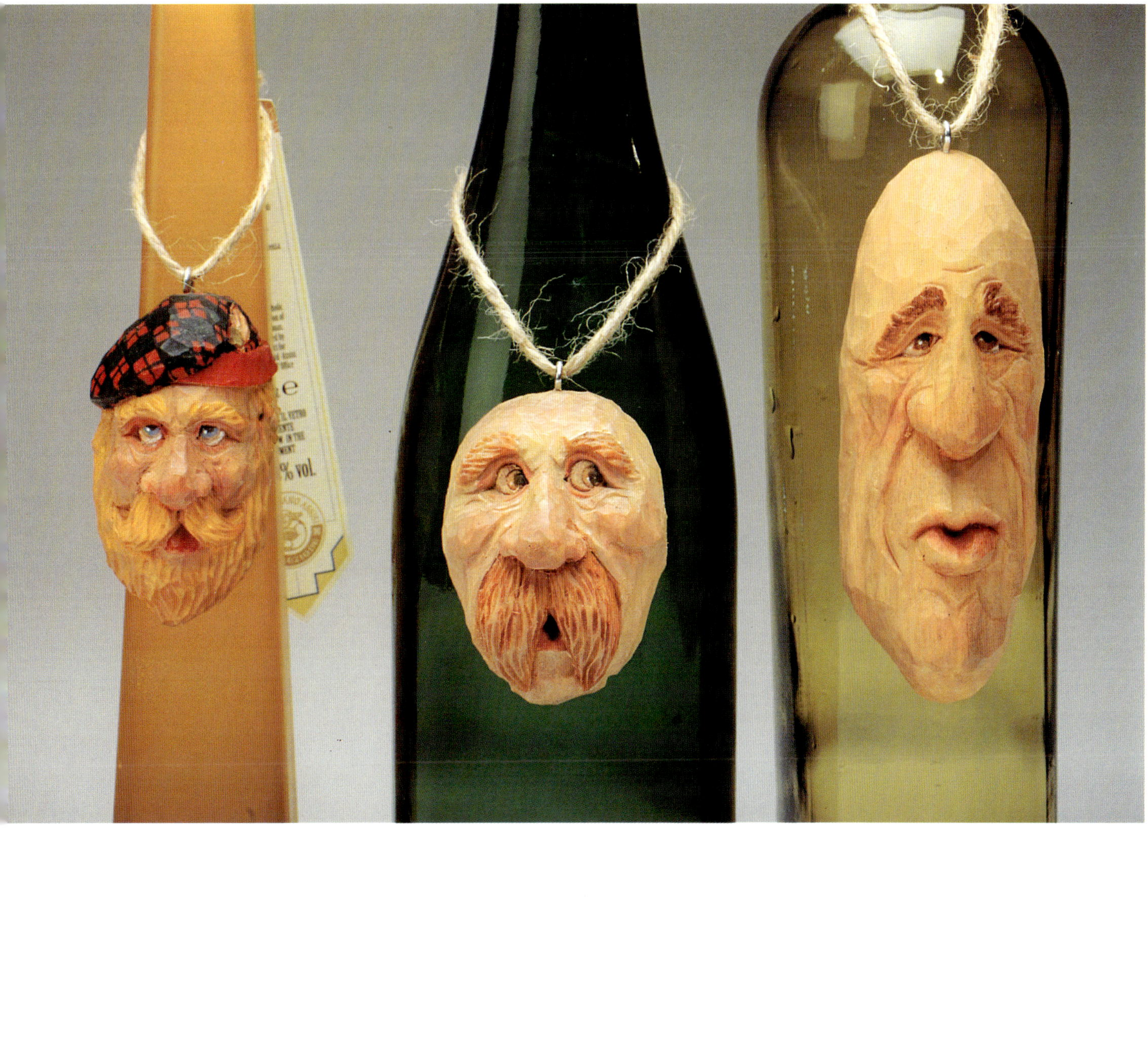

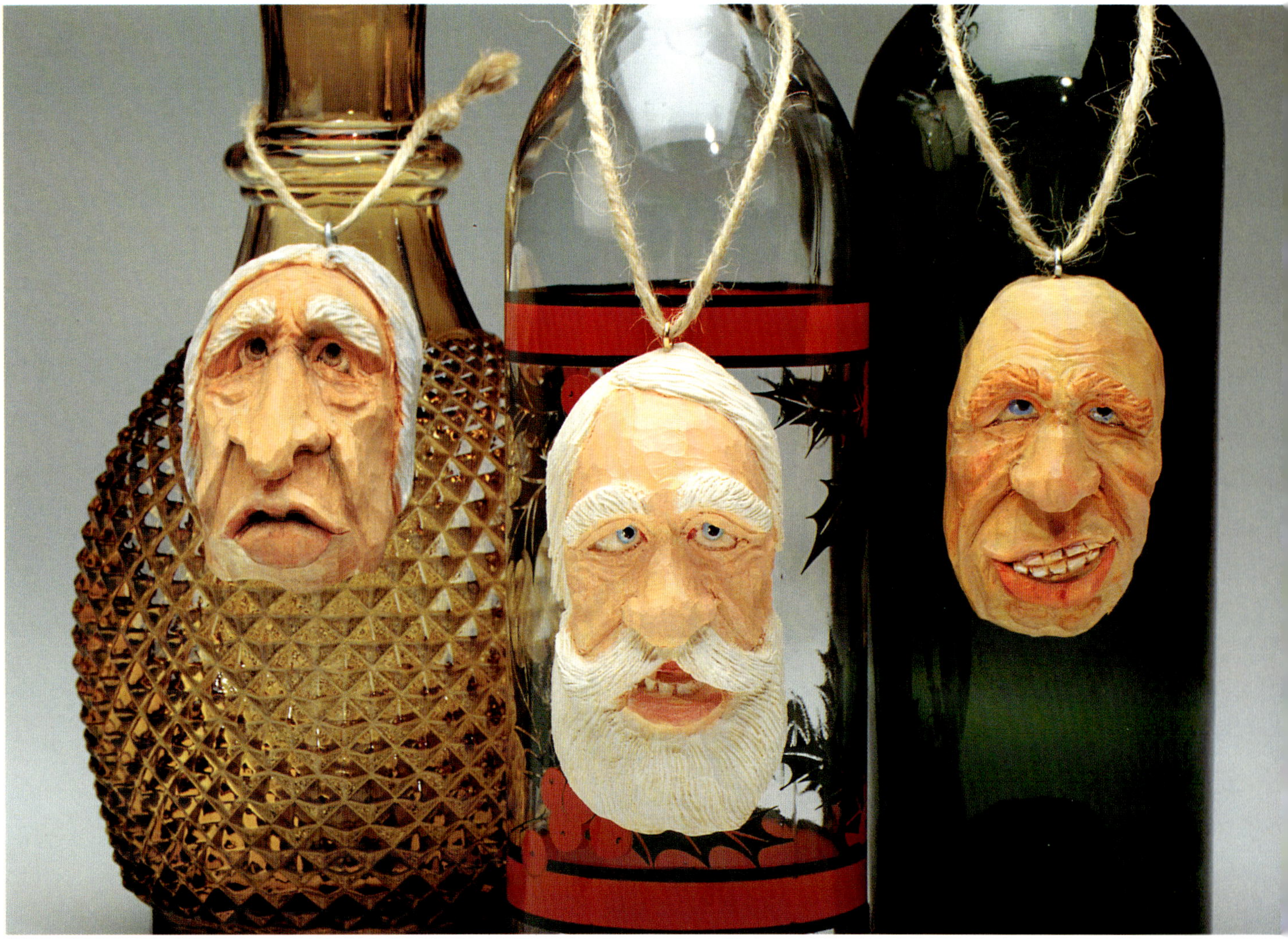

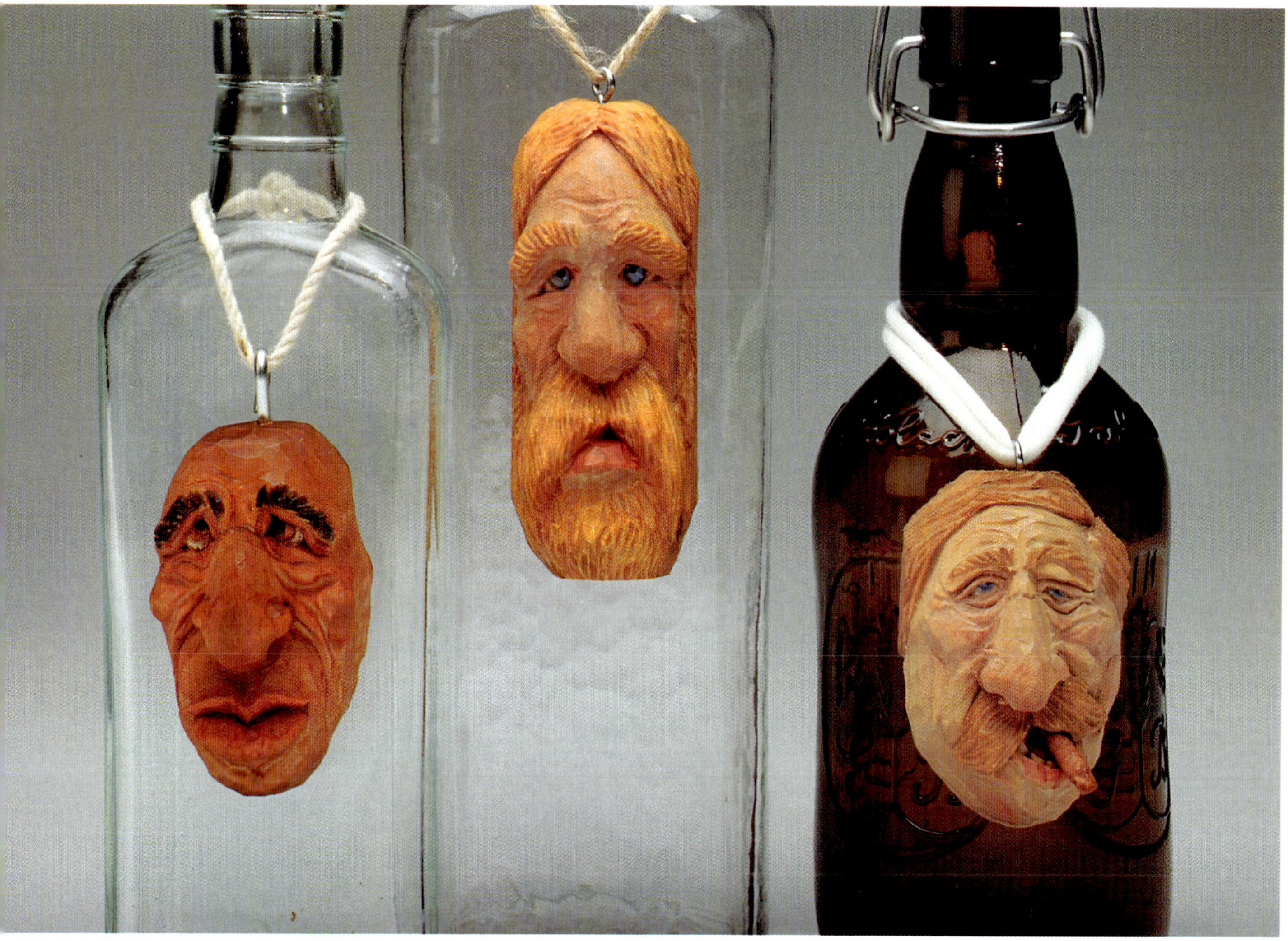

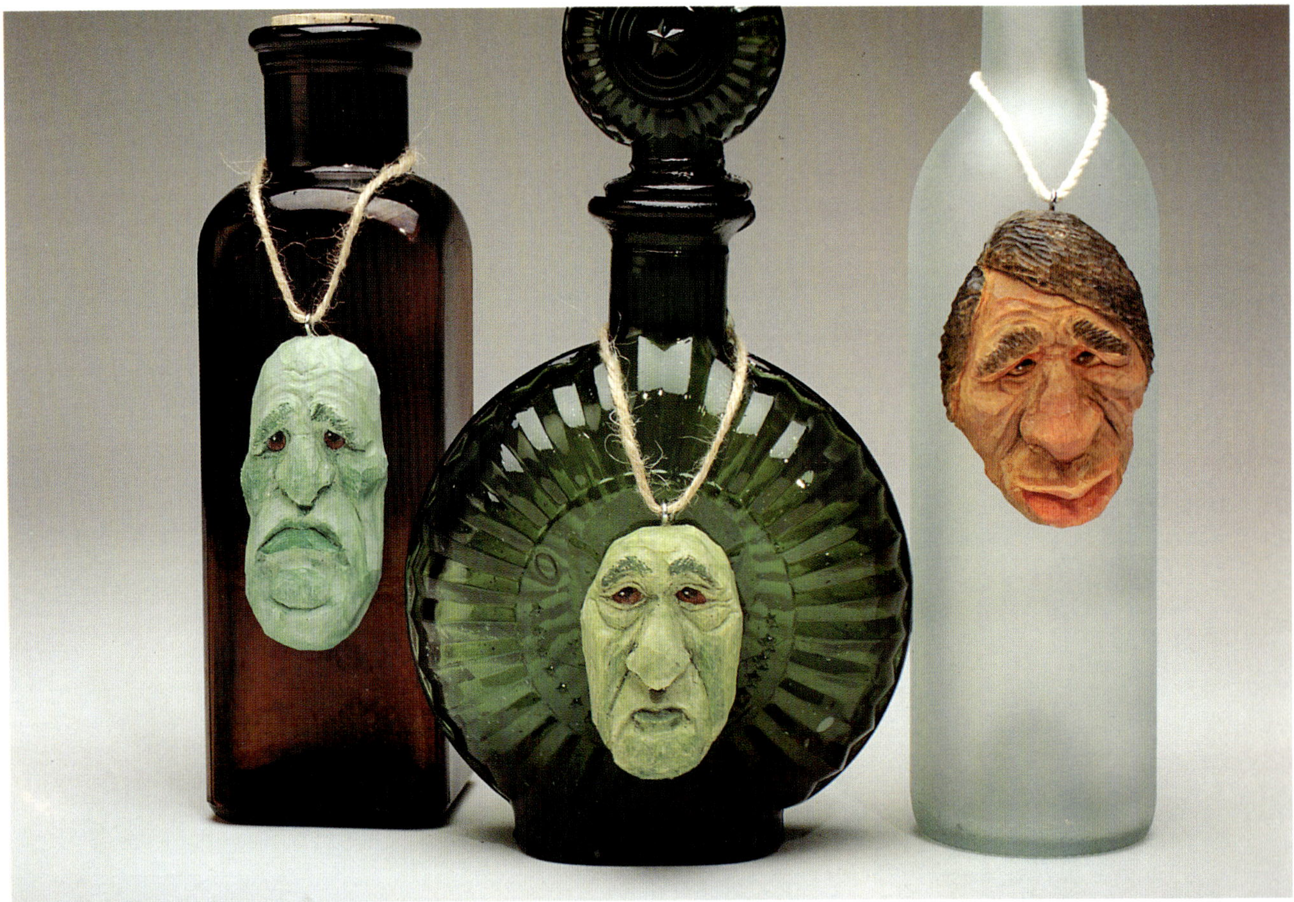

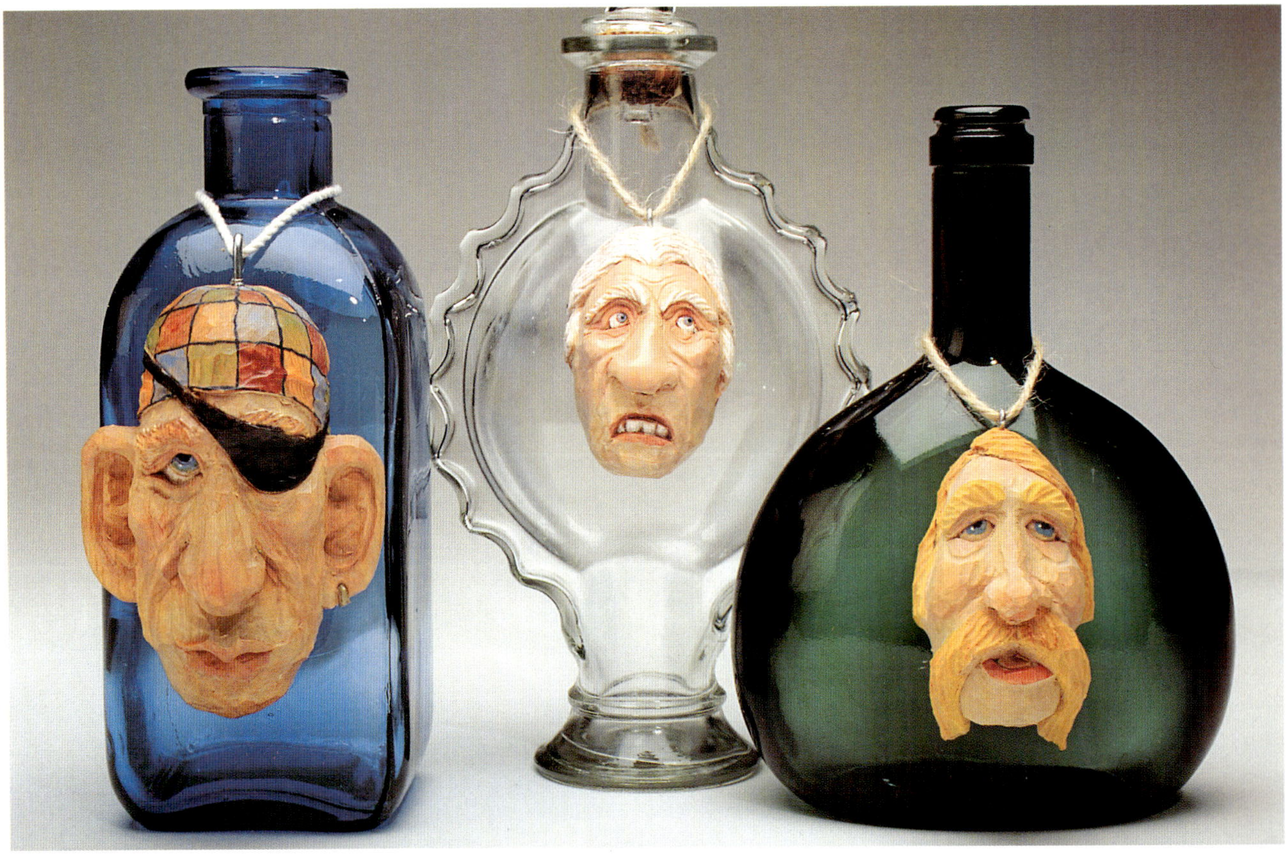

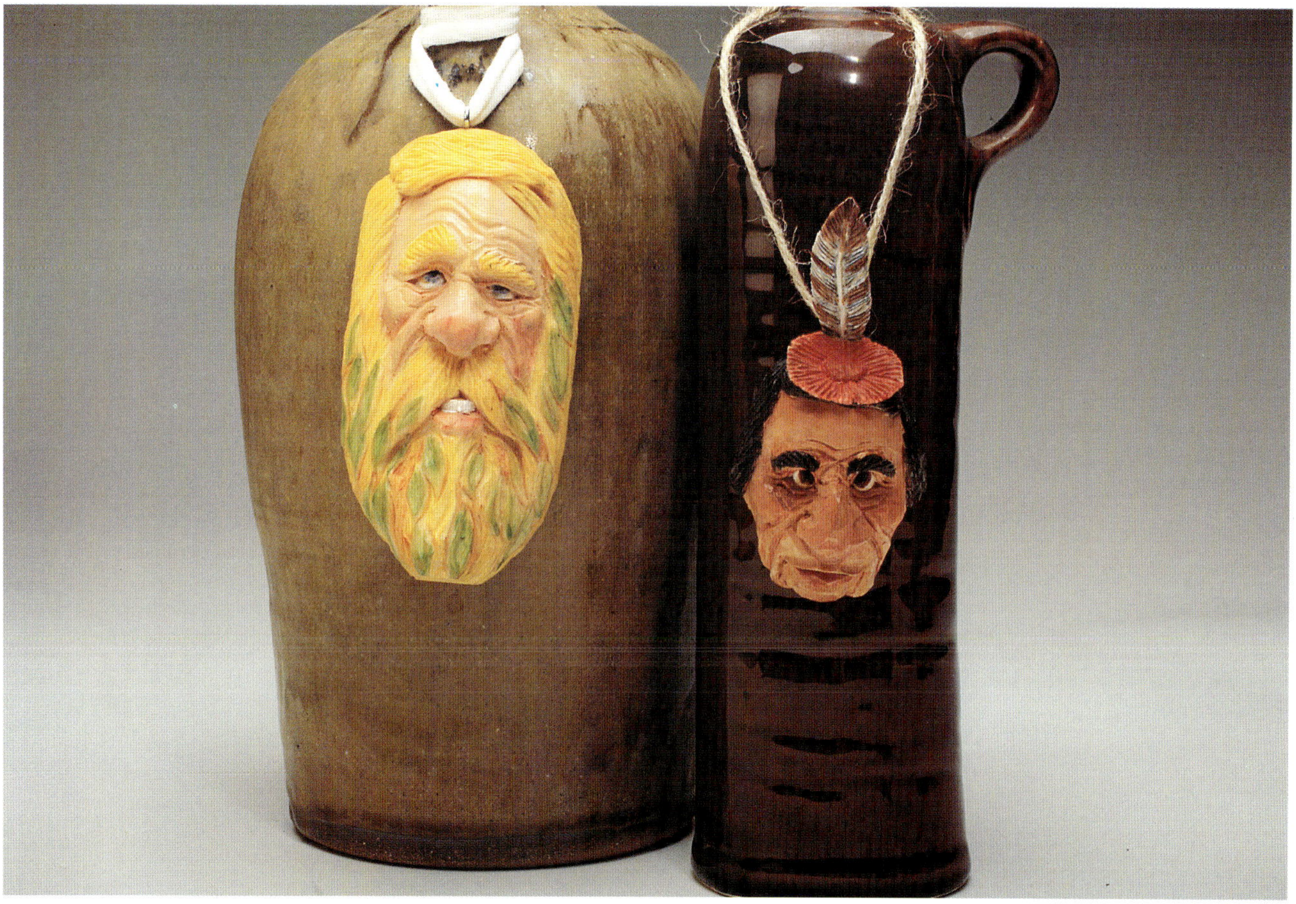

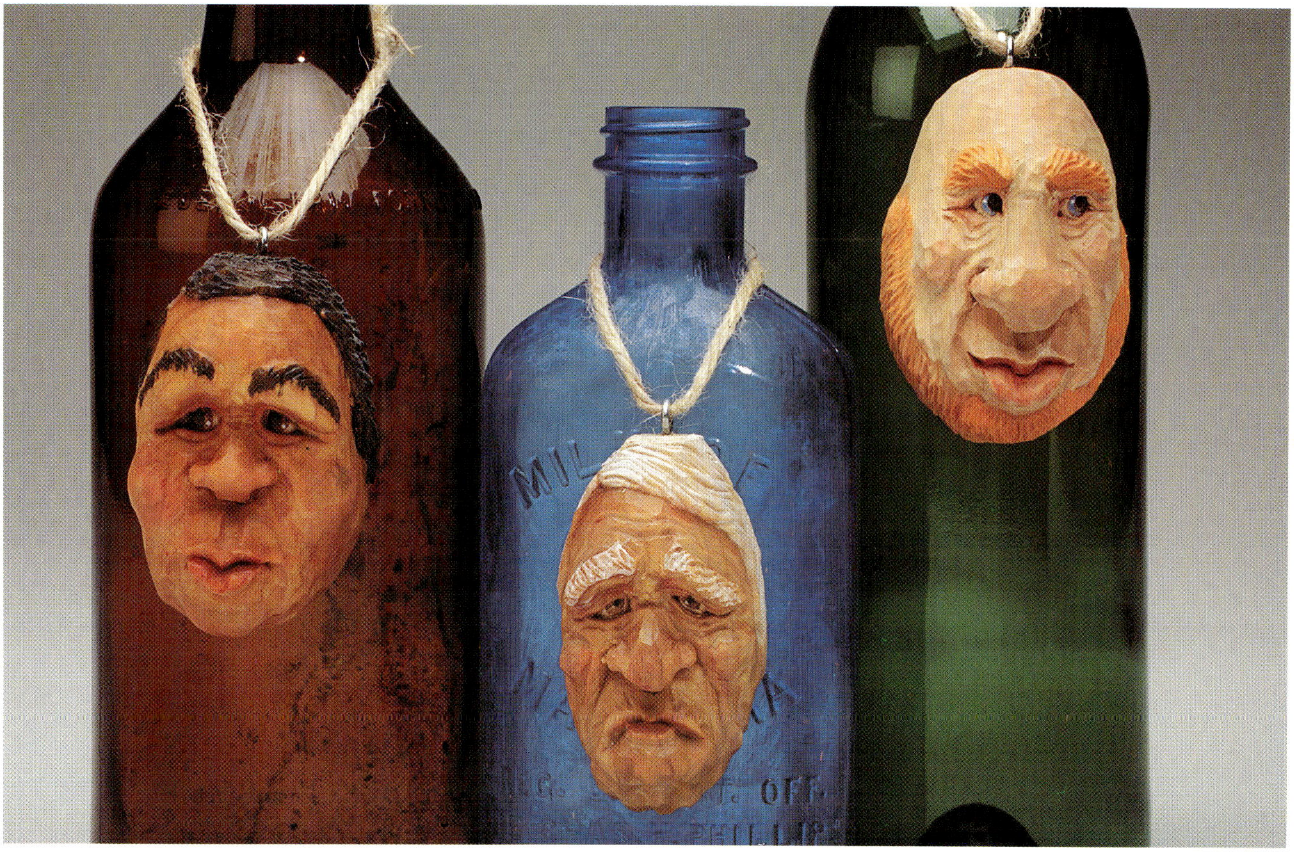

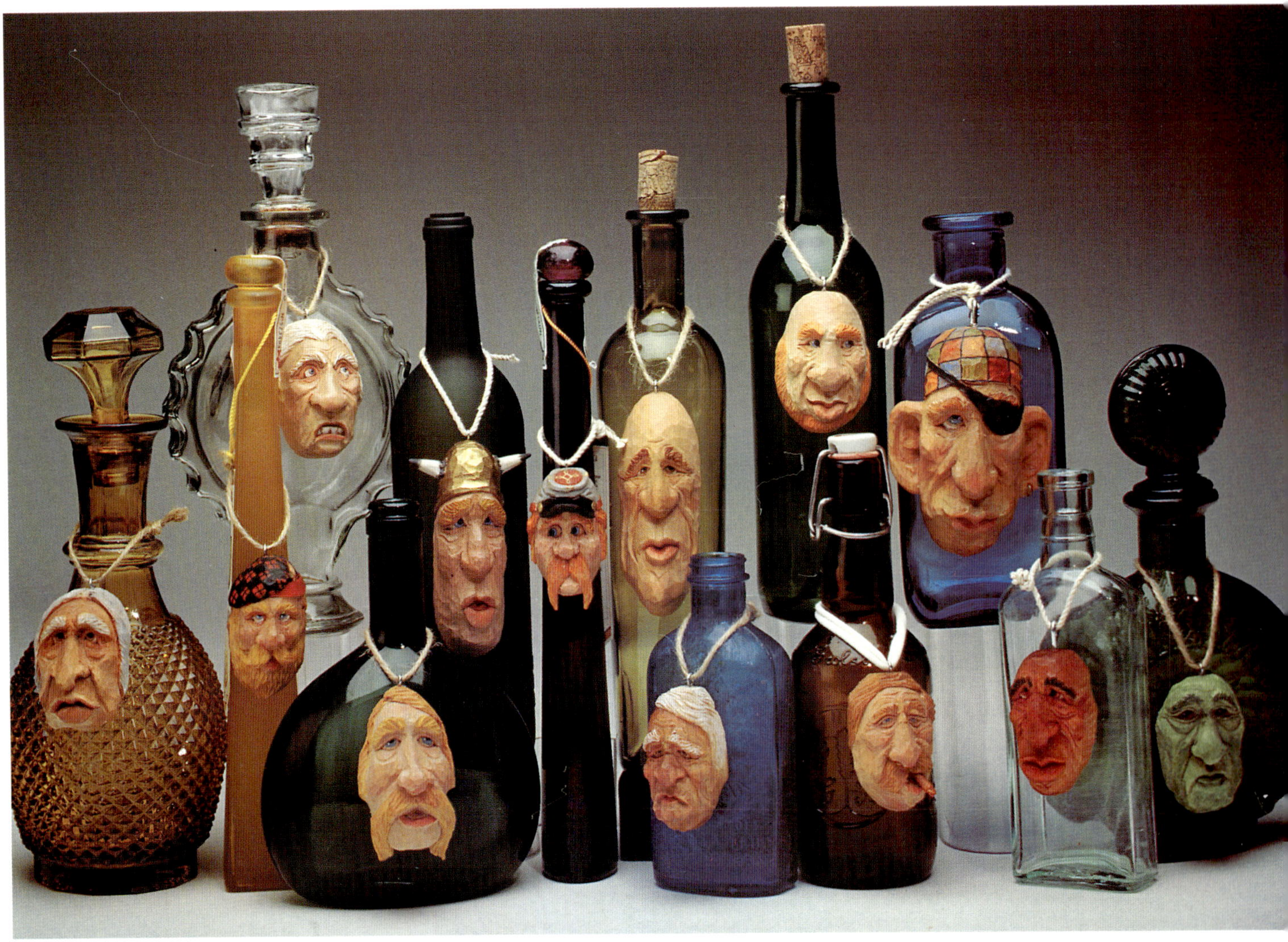